Applause

APPLAUSE

BOOK BY

Betty Comden and Adolph Green

MUSIC BY

Charles Strouse

LYRICS BY

Lee Adams

Based on the film ALL ABOUT EVE

and the original story by Mary Orr

RANDOM HOUSE · NEW YORK

FOR

Lauren Bacall

APPLAUSE *was first presented on March 30, 1970, by Joseph Kipness and Lawrence Kasha, in association with Neder- lander Productions and George M. Steinbrenner, III, at the Palace Theatre in New York City, with the following cast:*

(In order of appearance)

TONY AWARDS ANNOUNCER	John Anania
TONY HOST	Alan King
MARGO CHANNING	Lauren Bacall
EVE HARRINGTON	Penny Fuller
HOWARD BENEDICT	Robert Mandan
BERT	Tom Urich
BUZZ RICHARDS	Brandon Maggart
BILL SAMPSON	Len Cariou
DUANE FOX	Lee Roy Reams
KAREN RICHARDS	Ann Williams
BARTENDER	Jerry Wyatt
DANCER IN THE BAR	Sammy Williams
PETER	John Anania
BOB	Howard Kahl
PIANO PLAYER	Orrin Reiley
STAN HARDING	Ray Becker
DANNY	Bill Allsbrook
BONNIE	Bonnie Franklin
CAROL	Carol Petri
JOEY	Mike Misita
MUSICIANS	Gene Kelton, Nat Horne, David Anderson
TV DIRECTOR	Orrin Reiley
AUTOGRAPH SEEKER	Carol Petri

SINGERS: Sheilah Rae, Laurie Franks, Ernestine Jackson, Jeanette Seibert, Howard Kahl, Orrin Reiley, Jerry Wyatt, Henrietta Valor. DANCERS: Renee Baughman, Joan Bell, Debi Carpenter, Patti D'Beck, Marybeth Kurdock, Carol Petri, Bill Allsbrook, David Anderson, John Cashman, Nikolas Dante, Gene Foote, Gene Kelton, Nat Horne, Mike Misita, Ed Nolfi, Sammy Williams, Marilyn D'Honau, Jon Daenan.

The SINGERS and DANCERS appear as the FIRST-NIGHTERS, the BOYS, the GYPSIES, the GUESTS, and in various minor roles throughout the play.

Directed and choreographed by   Ron Field
Scenery by   Robert Randolph
Costumes by   Ray Aghayan
Lighting by   Tharon Musser
Musical direction & vocal arrangements by   Donald Pippin
Orchestrations by   Philip J. Lang
Dance and incidental music arranged by   Mel Marvin
Production Associate   Phyllis Dukore
Directorial Assistant   Otto Pirchner
Choreographic Assistant   Tom Rolla
Production Stage Manager   Terence Little

Synopsis of Scenes

The entire action takes place in and around New York.

Act One

Act Two

MUSICAL NUMBERS

ACT ONE

Overture

"Backstage Babble"	FIRST-NIGHTERS
"Think How It's Gonna Be"	BILL
"But Alive"	MARGO AND THE BOYS
"The Best Night of My Life"	EVE
"Who's That Girl?"	MARGO
"Applause"	BONNIE AND THE GYPSIES
"Hurry Back"	MARGO
"Fasten Your Seat Belts"	BUZZ, KAREN, HOWARD, BILL, DUANE, MARGO, AND THE GUESTS
"Welcome to the Theater"	MARGO

ACT TWO

"Inner Thoughts"	KAREN, BUZZ, AND MARGO
"Good Friends"	BUZZ, MARGO, AND KAREN
"The Best Night of My Life" (Reprise)	EVE
"She's No Longer a Gypsy"	DUANE, BONNIE, AND THE GYPSIES
"One of a Kind"	BILL AND MARGO
"One Hallowe'en"	EVE
"Something Greater"	MARGO AND BILL

x

Act One

(The Tony Awards)

The orchestra begins the overture, during which the
TONY AWARDS ANNOUNCER *says over a backstage microphone,
"Ladies and gentlemen, tonight we bring you, live, from
New York, the annual presentation of the Antoinette Perry
Awards for outstanding achievement in the theater." While
the orchestra continues playing, monitors on either side of
the proscenium and elsewhere throughout the theater show
silent filmed clips from a recent Tony Awards telecast, and
the stage is set as if the live audience is attending this very
event.*

*At the center of the stage is a white podium. A Tony
Awards seal forms its base, and behind it a large Tony
medallion hangs in the middle of the curtain. At some
point applause is heard, and the Tony Awards host, Alan
King, appears filmed on the monitors.*

ALAN KING *(On the monitors)*   From the applause, ladies
and gentlemen, we gather that the award to Lou Pacelli
for best actor in a supporting role was a popular one. And
now, to present the award for best actress in a starring
role, we proudly introduce two-time Tony winner, still
playing in the long-run hit *The Friendly Arrangement*,
that great lady of stage and screen, my good friend—
Margo Channing.

> *(MARGO CHANNING enters on stage, acknowledges
> the audience, and goes to the podium. Her image*

*appears at the same time on the monitors, in the
same action, and from now till the end of the scene
the action on the monitors is exactly the same as
what is happening on stage.* MARGO *is the essence
of the word "star"—arresting, elegant, and exuding
that rare, fast-disappearing quality, glamour)*

MARGO Thank you, thank you, ladies and gentlemen.
Well, here we are again, giving out the Tony Awards,
and I just heard the theater's all washed up. Now where
did I hear that? Oh, yes—from some big movie producer
whose office is now a used-car lot . . . Well . . . The
nominees for best actress in a starring role in a straight
play are Maureen Parker in *The Computer Next Door,*
Kelly Westbrook in *The Groupies,* Eve Harrington in
Somewhere to Love . . . *(A page enters)* and Julie
Sommers in *Figments.* And the winner is . . . *(The page
hands her an envelope. She opens it and reads)* Eve
Harrington!

(A spotlight hits EVE, *sitting in an aisle seat down
front in the theater. She springs up excitedly, looking startled and thrilled, and amidst applause, runs
up the steps to the stage. She rushes across to*
MARGO, *who graciously hands her the Tony and
steps aside. She is young and pretty but under her
breathless gratitude and humility, one can sense
that she knows exactly what she is saying and doing.
As she speaks,* MARGO *keeps looking at her with a
fixed public smile)*

EVE Oh, thank you, thank you. Needless to say, this is
the best night of my life! I have so many people to thank,
I hardly know where to begin. There's my director,

4

William Sampson; my author, Buzz Richards; my producer, Howard Benedict. But the one to whom I owe the most is . . . Margo Channing . . . not only a great actress, a legend in her own time, but the most generous, noble human being as well. I will never forget her. (EVE's *voice begins to fade, and the lights dim, except for a strong spotlight on* MARGO's *face*) As long as I live I will cherish the . . .

MARGO's VOICE (*Heard taped over the scene, as she stands unmoving, and with the same fixed smile on her face*) Goddamn it, Eve—I'm not dead yet! As a matter of fact, I feel more alive than ever. As I stand here, watching the audience drink you in, I am dumb-struck, filled with wonder and admiration. Can this dazzling vision be the same strange little mouse who pittered and pattered into my life on my opening night, just a year and a half ago? It can. It is. (EVE *has finished, takes a bow, and starts to move toward* MARGO) Oh, she's finished. What a lovely smile! Now kiss her on the cheek . . . (EVE *and* MARGO *are both in the spotlight. They kiss,* EVE *hiding* MARGO *from the audience*) Downstage cheek, dummy! You let her hide you! (EVE *passes in front of* MARGO *and goes off. The spotlight stays on* MARGO) Eve. Was it really less than two years years ago that we met? (MARGO *exits, and the lights go out. Her voice is still heard*) That night was not only the beginning of the theatrical season, it was the beginning of open season for *me*.

(*There is a close-up of her face, as if she were looking back into the past. The image ripples and fades as the curtain rises for the next scene*)

The scene is MARGO's *dressing room, right after her opening-night performance, a year and a half earlier than the preceding scene. Her dressing room is filled with telegrams, flowers and tumultuously babbling* FIRST-NIGHTERS. *It is a comfortable room, with armchairs, a small couch and a small bar. It can be divided by pulling a curtain across the center, leaving an area of privacy, stage left, with a dressing table, mirror, and exit to a bathroom. Also visible is an area just outside the dressing room door, stage right. The milling crowd fills the dressing room while others are pressing against the door trying to get in. The focal characters in this crowd scene are* HOWARD BENEDICT, *the urbane and forceful producer of this play and many others; the playwright* BUZZ RICHARDS, *eccentric and earthy-looking and a wild worrier; and* MARGO's *hairdresser, buddy, and confidante,* DUANE FOX. *The* FIRST-NIGHTERS *are engaged in the kind of excited babble that is typical of all big opening nights.*

FIRST-NIGHTERS (*Sing "Backstage Babble"*)
    Ba ba da, ba ba da,
    Ba ba da, ba ba da,
    Ba dom ba, da ba da,
    Ba dom ba, da ba da,
    Ba dom ba, da ba da.

    Ba ba da, ba da,

6

Ba ba da, wonderful,
Ba ba da, ba ba da,
Margo was just da da!

Ba ba da, she's lookin'
Mighty ba ba da,
Ba da ba, da ba wasn't she?

(BERT, *the stage manager, pushes through the crowd
with a fresh batch of telegrams which he puts into*
DUANE's *mouth, since both his hands are full, serving drinks.* DUANE *hands the drinks out, and exits
through the bathroom door*)

La da da, ba da Mr. Benedict,
Ba ba da, ba da ba,
Ba ba da, producer,
Ba ba da, ba da . . .

La la la,
Loved it, whoa whoa!

HOWARD   Bert, don't let any more people in. Too crowded
already.

(BERT *nods and exits*)

YOUNG WOMAN (*Ga-ga and full-bosomed, chirping at*
HOWARD, *who makes a note of her for the future*)
Hee bee dee bee dee bee dee bee dee,
Hee bee dee bee dee bee dee bee doo!

FIRST-NIGHTERS
Critics will certainly ba ba da,
Ba da ba, da ba doo!

BUZZ (*Approaching* HOWARD) What do you hear, Howard? Do you think they liked the play?

HOWARD They seem to like it okay, but we won't get reviews for an hour or so.

>   (BILL SAMPSON, *the director, enters from the dressing-room door*)

FIRST-NIGHTERS
> Didn't she ba ba da,
> Bee buh dee, marvelous!
> Ba da ba, da a hit!
> Look who directed it!
> Congratulations!

BILL (*Trying to work his way toward* HOWARD) Thanks!

FIRST-NIGHTERS
> Ba ba da, ba da.

WOMAN (*Stopping* BILL, *and gushing*)
> Dyah dyah, da da da,
> Dyah dyah, da da.

BILL Yeah, she sure was!

MAN (*Stopping* BILL *again*)
> Dyah dyah, da da da,
> Da da da dum!

BILL You can say that again.

8

FIRST-NIGHTERS
La la la la la la,
La la la la la la,
La da de da, just great!

(BILL *and* HOWARD *congratulate each other.* BUZZ
joins them, then they are again surrounded by the
FIRST-NIGHTERS)

Openings are really ba ba dah!
So exciting, ba ba da, ba da!
Lee bee dee bee doo bah dee bee,
Loved it very ba ba da!
Wasn't Margo ba ba da!
Thought the play was bee bee dee,
Sets and lights were bee bee dee,
What an uh-uh opening wow!

(*After the number,* MARGO *and* DUANE *enter from
her bathroom where she has been changing. She is
in her dressing gown. Everyone greets her; she and*
BILL *try to get together, but* FIRST-NIGHTERS *sur-
round her*)

MARGO   Bill!

WOMAN   Divine, Margo!

MARGO   How nice of you.

MAN   You're so witty.

MARGO   Thanks, but tell that to the author.

MAN   Miss Channing, I see everything you do.

MARGO   Oh, I hope not everything!

(BILL *and* MARGO *finally get together and embrace.* HOWARD *comes over to them*)

HOWARD   Nice work. Get yourself over to the party.

MARGO   I've just knocked myself out doing *this* show. Now I have to go over and do *that* one.

HOWARD   Get there.

MARGO   All right. But I want a minute with Bill before he leaves. Empty the room . . . diplomatically, of course.

HOWARD   Of course. Attention! *(They all listen to him)* Everybody—get the hell out! Margo will see you all at . the party.

FIRST-NIGHTERS *(Singing excitedly and exiting)*
  Ba ba da, marvelous!
  You were just ba ba da,
  Bee dee ba doo, sincere!
  Ra ba dee ba doo ba dee ba,
  Darling, get a cab . . .

YOUNG WOMAN *(Again directing her charms at* HOWARD)
  Thank you, Mr. Benedict,
  I doo ba da ba dee!

FIRST-NIGHTERS
  Ba ba da, terrific,
  Ba ba da, ba da ba,
  Da ba da ba, really,
  Ba ba da, ba da ba . .

> (*The* FIRST-NIGHTERS *and* HOWARD *exit.* BUZZ *sits
> on the sofa, busy with his telegrams.* DUANE *is comb-
> ing out a wig at the dressing table.* BILL *and* MARGO
> *are comparatively alone. The nature of their rela-
> tionship becomes immediately apparent. They are in
> love, but he is somewhat younger than she, and
> despite her surface confidence and sharpness, she is
> uncertain and touchingly vulnerable. He is, in ways,
> more mature than she, and tries to understand her
> hangups and patiently kid her out of them*)

BILL   Star, I have a few notes for you. (*She droops*) Ab-
solute perfection! . . . (*She glows and goes to him*) Except
you lost your biggest laugh in Act Two, dope, by moving
on your own line, and—

MARGO   (*Cutting and defensive*)   Listen, Herr Direktor,
since you've elected to abandon us tonight, I don't have
to take a goddamn thing from you. Who said you have
to do that idiotic movie in Rome?

BILL   *I* said. You keep forgetting some men have careers
just like women do. Expect me to give it all up? Slave
over a hot stove all day?

MARGO   I never heard of such a thing! You know actors
have to be watched like rotten kids. In a week the play
will fall apart . . . and so will I. Oh, Bill!

(*Collapsing, she runs to his arms as* KAREN, BUZZ's
wife, enters)

KAREN (*Excited*)   Bravo, Margo!

BUZZ (*Gets up from the sofa*)   Karen! I wish you'd sit next
to me on opening nights!

KAREN   How can I? You spend the whole time in the men's
room. (*Gives him his pills.* KAREN *is handsome, well-bred,
involved in the theater only through marriage, and still
full of girlish enthusiasms*). Buzz, did you hear the laughs
tonight? I never can believe those funny lines are written
by this undertaker I live with.

BUZZ   They come out of her mouth . . . (*Indicating* MARGO)
That's what makes them funny. (MARGO *bows to this*)
But there was one place in the second act—

(BILL *sits next to the dressing table*)

MARGO   Yes, yes, I know—I lost your biggest laugh. I'll
tell you about that line. I choke on it! It reminds me, *and*
the audience, I'm playing someone considerably younger
than myself.

BILL   You're sick, Margo.

MARGO   No—I'm forty.

(*She goes to the dressing table and sits.* BERT *re-
enters*)

BERT   Sorry about that late curtain in Scene Three, Margo.

(He hands some telegrams to KAREN *and exits)*

MARGO   Okay, Bert . . .

KAREN *(Enthusiastically)*   Listen, Margo . . . *(She goes over to* BILL *and hands him the wires)* I've been mingling. *The Friendly Arrangement* is a definite hit in the lobby, and the alley is full of fans just pouring love out at you.

MARGO   Love! Little beasts! All they care about is trading autographs. "I'll give you five Margo Channings for one Pearl Bailey." They've never even seen me on the stage.

KAREN   Well, one of them has. There's a girl out there who's seen every preview the whole three weeks. I brought her back here to meet you.

MARGO   What! Duane . . .

(She gestures to DUANE *to get rid of whoever it is. He moves toward the door, then stops as* KAREN *speaks)*

KAREN *(Crossing to* MARGO*)*   Wait! I've spotted her every night in the alley, half hidden in the shadows, and to-night she spoke up, and, Margo, this girl idolizes you! It's like something out of a book! You've *got* to—

BUZZ   Karen, on opening night!

KAREN *(Seriously pleading)*   She's spent her last penny to see you!

13

BILL Make her happy, Margo. Receive her and let her kiss your ring.

MARGO *(Gives in and gets up with a grand, satiric flourish)* Spent her last penny to see Margo Channing. The kid can't be all bad!

    (KAREN goes to the door and opens it. The men get up)

KAREN Come in, dear. *(It is EVE, looking quite different from the way she does in the Tony Awards scene. She is mousy and bedraggled, wearing a nondescript raincoat and pants)* Margo, this is Eve—Eve Harrington.

MARGO How do you do.

EVE *(Timid and awed, hanging back near the door)* How do you do.

MARGO And this is Mr. Sampson, Mr. Richards, and Duane Fox.

EVE Hello.

    (The men murmur hello's)

MARGO Won't you sit down?

EVE No, thank you, really. I'm just glad I have this chance to congratulate you all, and to thank you, Miss Channing, for lighting up my life—saving it, really.

MARGO *(Taken aback)* That's an extraordinary statement.

EVE *(Sincerely)* I mean it—literally. Seeing you on the stage changed everything for me.

MARGO Are you in the theater?

EVE Oh, I love the theater passionately. For years I belonged to our local dramatic society. We did Pinter and Albee. But I never gave any thought to being in it professionally.

MARGO *(Feeling she has done her duty, and moving back to the dressing table)* Oh.

BILL *(Politely)* Where was all this?

EVE Madison, Wisconsin. I grew up on a little farm near there. I used to try to escape from it into the world of my imagination—making up things, acting them out . . . Oh, what I'm saying is silly.

KAREN Please go on.

EVE Well, after school, I took a secretarial job. There I met someone wonderful who was also interested in theater. A dreamer, working in an office—like me. We got married. Soon enough the outside world woke us up. He was sent to Vietnam. I went to San Francisco to meet him on leave, then got the telegram that told me he was never coming back. Life was over for me. I went completely to pieces—dropped out, drifted aimlessly, half in a daze—hardly knowing who I was or what I was doing. I lost all contact with reality.

(They are all listening, spellbound. DUANE leaps up and breaks the mood)

DUANE   Wow! It's like being back in group therapy.

MARGO   Duane!

DUANE   Sorry.

EVE *(Continuing)*   I wound up in New York. One night, some kid I knew dragged me into a theater. I knew your movies, but it was the first time I'd ever seen you on the stage. I felt an energy and vitality . . . It was like suddenly walking into the sunlight again. I saw you every night until the play closed. I came back to life. *(Pauses)* I'm glad I've had this chance to tell you what you've meant to me. Good-bye.

MARGO *(Touched, gets up and takes EVE's hand)*   I think this is the nicest opening-night present I've ever had. Don't go, Eve. Stay around awhile.

BILL *(Gets up, as do all the others)*   Hey, I better get going.

MARGO *(Turning to Bill)*   Let me go to the airport with you!

BILL   We settled that already. I don't want to remember you in that neon light, with your mascara dripping into your shoes. Go to the party.

KAREN   We should be getting to that party. Come on, Buzz.

BUZZ   Wait for you, Margo?

MARGO   No, Duane'll drop me off.

KAREN   Good-bye, Bill. See you in three months. *Buona fortuna!*

BILL   *(Kissing her)*   *Grazie mille.* *(Shaking hands with* BUZZ*)* Pretty sneaky of me ducking out before the notices.

BUZZ   *(To* BILL*)*   Do you think they liked the play?

BILL   *(Shrugs)*   I don't know, but I did get an opinion from Max, the guy who sells orange juice in the lobby.

BUZZ   Well?

BILL   *(Making a thumbs-down gesture and raspberry sound)* He said theater today is action, participation, mass rape!

BUZZ   I don't think much of his orange juice, either.

KAREN   Good-bye, Eve.

EVE   Mrs. Richards, I'll never forget you.

KAREN   Good luck.

BUZZ   Good-bye, Miss Harrington.

EVE   Good-bye.
    *(*DUANE *opens the door.* BUZZ, KAREN, *and* DUANE *leave.* BILL *and* MARGO *are in each others arms.* EVE *turns and sees them)*

EVE (*Uncomfortably*)   I really should wait outside.

> (BILL *makes a little sound, indicating agreement.* EVE *leaves*)

MARGO   Oh, Bill!

BILL   Marry me when I get back.

MARGO (*Fencing*)   I'll think about it.

BILL   You've been thinking about it for two years.

MARGO   I'm a slow thinker.

BILL (*Turning to her, kidding, but trying to make a point*) Last chance to examine the merchandise! Classic profile, dazzling personality, talent, voted lover-of-the-year by his own high school. Aren't you afraid I'll be snapped up on the Via Veneto?

MARGO   Am I going to lose you?

BILL   Not a chance. I'll get you something beautiful in Rome.

MARGO   Just don't get your*self* something beautiful in Rome.

BILL (*He sings "Think How It's Gonna Be"*)

> Dry your pretty eyes,
> And let me have a smile,
> Think how it's gonna be
> When we're together again . . .

I don't want to go,
But planes come back, you know,
Think how it's gonna be
When we're together again . . .

Oh, we'll take a long, long walk,
Oh, we'll have a quiet talk,
Then just when the fire's low,
Honey, you know
Where we'll go . . .

So flash your famous smile,
The one that gets 'em all,
Think how it's gonna be,
Nothing but you and me!
Think how it's gonna be
When we're together again.

Hey, you know—I love you very much.

MARGO   I know. Hey, don't eat too much pasta. I want to
be able to get my arms around you when you come back.

BILL *(Singing)*

I don't want to go,
But planes come back, you know,
Think how it's gonna be,
Nothing but you and me!
Think how it's gonna be
When we're together again.

*(They stand looking at each other a moment and
then* BILL *exits.* DUANE *and* EVE *re-enter.* MARGO
goes to the dressing table and slumps dejectedly)

DUANE   Come on, Pagliacci, baby! Gotta get prettied up for the party!

EVE   And I should be getting back to my room.

MARGO   What! The girl who sat through this play twenty-four times? You're coming to the party!

EVE   Oh, I couldn't! I'd be so . . . uncomfortable!

MARGO   (*Getting up*)   *You'd* be uncomfortable? How do you think I feel? Everyone glued to TV sets, huddled over advance copies of *The Times*, waiting for the poison gas to creep over the room . . . How'll I ever get through it without Bill? (*A sudden inspiration*) I know! I won't go!

DUANE   *What?*

MARGO   Well, I deserve a good time tonight! (*Filled with a new energy*) Duane, how'd you like to escort two lonely ladies out on the town?

DUANE   I've got a date.

MARGO   Bring him along.
         (*She goes over to the closet to start changing.* DUANE *follows, and holds the dressing robe in front of her so she can dress behind it*)

DUANE   I was just going down to the Village—join some friends. I don't know if you'll like it.

MARGO (*Taking a dress from the closet and getting into it*)
We'll adore it. Eve, we're going to the Village!

EVE   But it's opening night. You must feel exhausted!

MARGO   I'm too exhausted to go to the party . . . but I'm
much too excited to go home to sleep! (MARGO *is finished
dressing. Revitalized and ready to take off, she sums up
her feelings of that evening to* EVE *and* DUANE, *singing
"But Alive"*)

I feel groggy and weary
And tragic,
Punchy and bleary
And fresh out of magic,
But alive,
But alive,
But alive!

I feel twitchy and bitchy
And manic,
Calm and collected
And choking with panic,
But alive,
But alive,
But alive!

I'm a thousand diff'rent people,
Ev'ry single one is real,
I've a million diff'rent feelings,
Okay, but at least I feel!

And I feel rotten
Yet covered with roses,
Younger than springtime

And older than Moses,
Frisky as a lamb,
Lazy as a clam,
Crazy, but I am
Alive!

(*During this last verse, she links arms with* EVE *and* DUANE *and they come downstage as the set changes behind them. The sound of discotheque music is heard*)

The scene is a bar in Greenwich Village. A wall of colored, blinking lights descends downstage as the three dance off. As the wall is pulled up, it forms a ceiling; two side walls and a back wall fly in. The right wall is lined with bottles, as in a bar, and a rolling bar is then pushed on to the stage in front of the wall, while the rest of the bar set flies in. A large, lighted jukebox is rolled on.

The walls are covered with posters and large photographs of movie idols—mainly Paul Newman, Judy Garland and Marlon Brando.

The place is filled with people, all of them dancing, and it becomes apparent that all of them are male, dressed in varied flamboyant attire. MARGO, *followed by* EVE *and* DUANE, *enters. Suddenly the action freezes and, stunned, the* BOYS *stare at* MARGO.

BOYS *(In one breath)*   Margo Channing!

MARGO   Drat! I've been recognized!

BARTENDER   But I can't believe it. Here! I mean, didn't you open tonight? The Buzz Richards play?

MARGO   Guilty.

BARTENDER *(Overcome)*   This is a historic moment. We light candles in front of your picture!

(They are still frozen, gaping at her)

MARGO   Duane, I'm spoiling the fun.

DUANE   Shall I call the party and tell them you'll be there soon?

TWO BOYS   Don't go!

BARTENDER   Please stay!

MARGO *(Making up her mind on the spot)*   Silly boys . . . I'm here for the night! *(Without analyzing it, she feels relaxed and safe in this atmosphere of total adoration and no competition. She begins singing "But Alive" again)*

> I feel wicked and whacky
> And mellow,
> *(Gives her cape to DUANE)*
> Firm as Gibraltar
> And shaky as jello,
> But alive,
> But alive,
> But alive!
>
> I feel half Tijuana,
> Half Boston,
> Partly Jane Fonda
> And partly Jane Austen,
> But alive,
> That's the thing!
> But alive!

BOYS *(Speaking at the same time)* Miss Channing! . . .
Pleased to meet you! . . . You're great! . . . Margo! . . .
Love you . . .

MARGO
This kaleidoscope of feelings
Whirls around inside my brain,
I admit I'm slightly coo-coo
But it's dull to be too sane . . .

And I feel brilliant and brash
And bombastic,
Limp as a puppet
And simply fantastic!
But alive,
But alive,
But alive!

(MARGO *dances with the* BOYS, *uninhibited, exub-
erant and free)*

BOYS
She's here, my dear, can you believe it!
She's here, oh, God, I can't believe it!
She's here! It's just too groovy to believe!

MARGO, DUANE, EVE and BOYS
This kaleidoscope of feelings
Whirls around inside my brain,
We admit we're slightly coo-coo,
But it's dull to be too sane!

Love, love . . . love, love, love . . .
(They clap)

MARGO *(Leaping on top of the jukebox)*
I feel brilliant!
Bombastic!
Super!
Fantastic!

> *(Seven* BOYS *leap up on the jukebox, surrounding her. When they jump off, she has disappeared. She reappears from behind the jukebox)*

Alive . . .
Alive . . .
Alive!

BOYS   Margo!
> *(She dances more and more wildly with the* BOYS. *They fling her back and forth, and she winds up in a pose on* DUANE'S *shoulder. Then she kisses one of the* BOYS *(*SAMMY*) good-bye and, as the music picks up and the wall of flashing lights descends, she leaves with* DUANE *and* EVE*)*

Blackout

BOYS *(To* SAMMY*)*   Let's go.

SAMMY *(Pushing them away and starting to follow)*   I love her. I mean I really love *her! (The* BOYS *pick him up and carry him off, while he protests, screaming)* Margo! Margo! Margo!

Blackout

SCENE FOUR

The scene is MARGO's *living room, still later that evening.*
This set has four playing levels. It is an interesting,
lived-in room, filled with theater memorabilia, pictures, etc.
MARGO's *Tony is set on a glass coffee table in the center*
of the stage, just in front of a light-colored sofa.

There is a corridor on the right leading off to the kitchen.
At the base of the right wall is a half-round cabinet on
which sits a lamp and the phone. The wall is covered with
pictures, and there is a set of double doors leading to the
outside. There are some steps and a railed landing leading
to MARGO's *bedroom, the entrance to which is upstage and*
to the right.

In the center of the back wall are double doors to the
library. To the right of these doors is a table covered with
pictures; to the left, an open bar with two backless bar-
stools underneath.

The lowest playing level is in the central stage area.
To the right of the sofa is a comfortable swivel chair.
Upstage and to the left of the sofa are two steps to the
terrace.

Five open perpendicular panels on the left wall are win-
dows, the panels extending into the ceiling like an artist's
skylight.

As the lights come up, DUANE *is at the bar pouring a*
drink. EVE *is standing on the steps to the right, looking up*
at the pictures on the back-wall table.

EVE (*Excited*) Laurence Olivier! Noël Coward! (*Goes to*

the coffee table in front of the sofa and picks up the Tony Award) And her Tony Award! I've never seen one close up!

(*DUANE moves to the terrace and sits*)

DUANE (*Flatly*) Very few have.

(*The phone rings.* DUANE *"oh's" and gestures that he's too far away to get to it.* EVE *looks hesitant a moment, then goes and picks it up. She has the Tony with her and puts it down next to the phone*)

EVE Oh! I'll get it. Uh . . . Miss Channing's residence.

BUZZ'S VOICE Hello, Service, this is Buzz Richards again. She still . . . ?

EVE Oh, it's Eve, Mr. Richards—Eve Harrington. We met backstage.

BUZZ'S VOICE Oh, yeah. We've been calling everywhere. Where the hell's she been?

EVE Well, she went out dancing with Duane and me.

BUZZ'S VOICE We were ready to kill her till we read the notices.

EVE The notices! Were they . . . ?

BUZZ'S VOICE All terrific. She got two "glowings," three "brilliants," and one "incandescent."

EVE (*Happily*) She's just changing. I'll call her and—

BUZZ'S VOICE No, no! I'm in a street booth. Just tell her God has been good to us. By that I mean *The New York Times.*

EVE Good night. (*As she hangs up,* MARGO *enters from the bedroom in pajamas and a robe, carrying her slippers.* DUANE *gets up*) That was Mr. Richards! They've been calling and calling. The reviews . . .

    (DUANE *moves off the terrace as* MARGO *comes down the steps*)

MARGO (*Apprehensively*) "The reviews"!

EVE They said you were glowing, brilliant, incandescent!

MARGO Lovely! What did they say about Bill?

EVE It was great for everybody.

MARGO We're a hit!

    (*She tosses her slippers gleefully in the air; they land behind the couch.* DUANE *and* MARGO *hug each other*)

DUANE Good! Now I can buy that fun fur I've been laughing at! I'll put the water on for your Sanka. (*Starts to leave, then stops*) Put on your slippers!

    (*He goes for them, but* EVE *moves ahead of him*)

EVE I'll get them!

(DUANE *looks at her a moment, a little uneasily then* *exits.* EVE *brings them over to* MARGO, *who is sitting* *on the terrace wall, next to the steps)*

MARGO   Thank you, dear. Tonight's been fun, hasn't it?

(*She puts on the slippers*)

EVE   Fun? (*She sings "The Best Night of My Life" with* *great simplicity*)

The best night of my life
Is here, is now.
Knowing you has got to be
The greatest thing that ever happened to me.

If I could freeze this moment,
And take it home with me,
I would—I would,
But time goes by,
And, oh,
I know that I
Never can live
This moment again,
This moment again . . .

The best night of my life,
The best night of my life,
Don't go, don't go . . .

There's no way to say thank you,
It wouldn't come out right.
But . . . thank you
For the best night of my life.

(MARGO, *touched, gets up and goes to* EVE *to thank her.* DUANE *enters*)

DUANE   The water's boiling. We better cut out. Our go-go girl has got to get her rest. (MARGO *sits on the sofa*) Can I drop you someplace, Eve?

EVE (*A little too eagerly*)   I know! Instead of Sanka, I wish you'd let me fix you one of our hometown toddies. It'll help you sleep.

MARGO   That sounds nice, Eve.

EVE   It'll only take a minute. Good night, Duane.

(*She exits to the kitchen*)

DUANE (*Crossing to the TV set, turns it around, and on*) Okay, now watch the late movie, drink your "hometown toddy," and get to sleep. (*Kisses her on the head*) Good night, sweetheart, you really were something tonight! I'm going to light a candle in front of your picture my*self!*

(*He goes to the door*)

MARGO   Thanks, but let's not forget—without your magic fingers in my hair, I'd be nothing!

(DUANE *blows a kiss and exits.* MARGO *is on the couch, relaxed. A voice from the TV set fills the room. It is* MARGO'S *voice, from an old movie*)

3 1

MARGO'S VOICE *(From the TV set)* Tomorrow I have to please General Von Schteichler. That's war. Tonight I just want to please you. That's—

MARGO *(Leaping up, disgustedly)* Good God, another Margo Channing Festival! *(Takes off her robe and gets up to turn off the set)* There I am again!

> *(As* MARGO *is turning down the sound,* EVE *enters with the drink)*

EVE *(In front of the sofa)* Oh, don't turn it off! *Victory at Dawn!* Leave the picture on, *please! (The sound is off. They both look at the picture)* I know just what Dana Andrews is saying! *(With a great deal of expression, as she stares at the set)* "Some day this war will be over, and the boys will come back home—Izzy, Pat, Sam, and Angelo—together again under a crazy blanket of red, white, and blue." And you say, "Oh, Terry, Terry," and then he says—

MARGO Never mind what he says. I need that drink. *(Takes the toddy and sips it, looking unbelievingly at herself on the screen)* Look at her! *(Sits)* She was nineteen years old and a big blinding movie star. That year Bill Sampson fell in love with her. He was twelve. He worshipped her from afar . . . *(Gets up)* from a second balcony in Jersey City. In love with a shadow.

> *(She drinks)*

EVE Now . . . I'm sure he loves you for what you are.

MARGO Yes, but what *are* I? Hey! What's in this drink? And which one does he want to marry? Margo today?

(The refrain of "But Alive" is played lugubriously. She sinks down in the sofa in a schlumpfy pose) Margo on stage? *(The refrain of "But Alive" is played glamorously. She takes a woman-of-the-world pose)* Or that one! *(She points to the set)* Miss Eternal Second Balcony! *(She sticks out her tongue at her image on the screen, then sings "Who's That Girl?")*

Who's that girl
With the permanent wave
And the dress below her knees?
Who's that doll
In the open-toed pumps,
Would you kindly tell me, please?

Look at her,
Miss Nineteen Forty-six!
Teen-age Margo,
Queen of the forties' flicks,
Mellowrooney!

Who's that girl
With the Maybelline eyes,
Acting like she knew the score?
Ixnay, Daddy-o,
I never saw that girl before!
Who's that girl with the
Permanent grin
And the stockings with the seams?
Did that kid with the caps on her teeth
Launch a million G.I.s' dreams?

Where is she,
That girl of yesterday?

33

With her falsies,
Leading Lew Ayres astray!
Boogie-woogie baby!

Who's that girl
With the chic shoulder pads,
Could it be that long ago?
Nosirreebob,
Fooryackasackee,
She isn't anyone I know!

> (MARGO *begins to dance some mid-forties jitterbug
> steps and pulls up* EVE *to join her, spinning her
> around and back a few times till* EVE *falls back into
> a chair, laughing*)

Watch her dance,
You can tell that she's hep,
'Cause she digs that jumpin' jive!
Wind her up,
And she really can act,
You would swear that she's alive!

How she smokes
Those brand-new filter tips!
Watch her pucker
Those red-hot Tangee lips!
Hey-bob-a-ree-bob!

Who's that girl
In the platform heels,
Who could that tomato be?

That snazzy chick,
Floy doy, floy doy!
Truckin' on down
Tuxedo junction . . .

EVE *(Singing)*
   In the pin-striped suit,

MARGO
   And the upswept hair!
   Boogie-woogie bugle boy from Company B!
   Knock, knock . . .

EVE
   Who's there?

MARGO
   Me!
   Hubba hubba!

>   *(To finish the number,* MARGO *strikes a glamorous
>   movie-star pose, then exits up the stairs and into her
>   bedroom, popping out again for a last wave and
>   then in again.* EVE *crosses to the TV to turn it off.
>   As she does so, the phone rings. She rushes to get
>   the phone on the first ring)*

EVE   Hello? . . . A friend. Eve Harrington . . . Oh! Mr.
   Benedict . . . She's just gone up to her bedroom . . . I
   think she's going to sleep. Late reviews all good? . . .
   I'll tell her in the morning . . . *(With a secret smile)* Oh,
   yes—I'll be here. (EVE *hangs up. She sees the Tony standing there and picks it up. Holding it in front of her in
   both hands, she takes it and turns to face the audience.
   She sings as the light dims)*

   So thank you
   For the best night of my life!

SCENE FIVE

The scene is Margo's dressing room, four months later.
HOWARD, PETER, MARGO'S *agent, and* BOB, *her lawyer, are*
engaged in a heated argument.

HOWARD   No, no, no. Tell your client, forget it!

PETER   But Howard . . . !

HOWARD   If she takes next week off, she can take off forever! I'll tear up her two-year contract!

BOB   Howard!

HOWARD   The play's running nearly four months, and I
know what kind of hit I've got! I don't need her.

PETER   You're bluffing. Those benefit ladies bought *Margo*.
Without her, they'll cancel!

(BUZZ *bursts into the room, desperate, frantic. He*
hurries over to HOWARD)

BUZZ   Hey! What's this I hear—Margo wants to go to
Rome! Close the show!

HOWARD   Christmas week!

BUZZ I know Bill's stuck there doing that picture, but—

PETER She's only human.

BUZZ *I'm* only human! The bottom will fall out of the show . . . and out of my new country house! Japanese rock garden! Swimming pool! Cesspool!

HOWARD *(To the group)* Look, is it my fault she insists on being faithful? *Tough.* Let her go jog around the reservoir till he comes back.

(DUANE *enters*)

DUANE She'll be offstage in a minute, gentlemen.

(BOB *goes to the bar for a drink and* BUZZ *joins him.* PETER *goes to the sofa*)

HOWARD *(Offhandedly)* Duane, when did the Empress first think up this brilliant plan?

DUANE I'm in charge of what goes *on* her head, not what's in it.

HOWARD Come on—you're her Prime Minister, you've got her ear.

DUANE Someone else has her ear now. I'm just a simple peasant again, busy with my pin curls.

HOWARD You know plenty. I'll take an option on your first play.

(MARGO *sweeps in, wearing a glamorous pailletted evening gown, followed by* EVE. EVE *now looks less mousy, in a trim, simple dress*)

MARGO (*Over-heartily*) Hello, gentlemen!

HOWARD Hello, Margo.

MARGO Oh, Eve, were you watching? I got that laugh back in the last scene!

EVE I know.

MARGO She's terrific! She pointed out to me that Emerson has been upstaging me and—

HOWARD (*Kisses her hand briskly and moves to leave*) Excuse me, Margo, but I must go.

MARGO (*Looking around at all of them*) Oh. Then it's all settled?

HOWARD (*Turning*) Margo, it's out of the question.

MARGO (*Tightening*) Oh?

HOWARD You're going mad.

MARGO You're a mind reader. If I don't see Bill soon, I'm going to be a very . . . sick . . . lady

HOWARD Don't threaten me with that nervous-breakdown crap. You're about as fragile as a moose!

MARGO *(Suddenly very convincingly on the verge of tears and trembling)* It's . . . not a threat. I'm about to collapse.

(She looks very faint)

HOWARD *(Gently, with great sympathy)* Oh, Margo, I didn't realize. The public will understand. I'll just post a notice saying, "Show closed on account of a cold spell . . . *(Suddenly turning on her violently)* and hot pants!"

(MARGO is furious)

MARGO Disgusting! I don't talk to you any more! I'm going to be on the plane next Sunday!

PETER But sweetie, be realistic!

BOB You've got a contract with Howard!

MARGO *(To BOB)* And you represent both of us. I need someone on *my* side. Buzz?

BUZZ *(Uncomfortably on the spot)* Geeeee, Margo . . .

MARGO *(Mimicking him)* Geeeee, Buzz, you'd starve without those royalties for the week! Eve! Tell them I'm right.

(MARGO looks at them triumphantly, but EVE is silent. MARGO looks at her)

EVE *(Quietly)* I can't. I'm really thinking of you. Mr.

Sampson is so busy, you wouldn't have any time together, and you might feel you were just in the way. (MARGO *is taken aback, and stares at* EVE) And . . . all those people . . . coming in Christmas week, expecting to see Margo Channing . . .

MARGO (*After a long pause*) As I said, it's a rotten idea, and how dare you try to talk me into it!

HOWARD (*Relieved*) Margo, you're a pro. (*They kiss*) That's show business.

MARGO (*Flatly, snapping her fingers*) Hey, I wish I'd said that.

> (*She exits into the bathroom,* DUANE *following.* PETER *and* BOB *exit*)

EVE (*Picking up her notebook and approaching* HOWARD) Oh, Mr. Benedict, now that you're here . . . (*Starts reading from her notes in a business-like fashion*) Spotlight man's been drinking again. I've reported it to the union, but I'm afraid no one but you can do anything about it. Miss Channing's second-act shoes came back dyed the wrong color. She's very unhappy and must have another pair. We sent you a note about it a week ago.

HOWARD (*Admiringly*) Well, I hope she's paying you plenty. You're certainly worth it.

EVE Thank you.

BUZZ (*Moves toward* EVE *as* HOWARD *goes to the door*) Would you tell Margo we hope she'll come up to the country this weekend? Karen told me you were something kind of special. Right, as usual.

EVE   And she told me at lunch your new play is kind of special. She says it's the best thing you've ever written.

BUZZ   She says that about everything I write—even my tax returns. (*Starts to leave*) Coming, Howard?

HOWARD (*Who has been watching* EVE, *intrigued*)   Yes. Good night.

> (BUZZ *and* HOWARD *exit.* DUANE *enters, holding the pailletted evening dress, followed by* MARGO, *who has changed into street clothes. He gives the dress to* EVE, *goes to the closet, puts on his coat, then takes out* MARGO's)

EVE   Mr. Richards hopes you'll come to Connecticut this weekend.

MARGO (*Wistfully*)   Instead of Rome—exotic Westport. Coming, Eve?
> (MARGO *walks toward the door.* EVE *examines the dress*)

EVE   A couple of these paillettes are loose. I'll just stay a minute and tack them in place.

MARGO   Thank you, dear.

EVE (*Stopping her*)   Miss Channing, I'm sorry.

MARGO   You only said what you thought was right. Good night.

(DUANE *looks at* EVE, *then he and* MARGO *go out, closing the door*)

DUANE (*Stopping* MARGO, *on the other side of the door*) Margo, ever hear of the union?

MARGO   Yes, we won the Civil War.

DUANE   I mean the *wardrobe* union. She's not supposed to do *that*, too.

(*He points toward* EVE. *Inside the room, she is holding* MARGO'*s costume against her body, looking at herself in the mirror and bowing like a triumphant star*)

MARGO   Oh, of course, I'll tell her. (*She opens the door, re-entering the dressing room, and sees what* EVE *is doing. She is taken aback, but recovers in a second*) Eve! (EVE *wheels around, whipping the dress aside*) I think you'd better let wardrobe take care of the wardrobe.

EVE (*Composed*)   Of course. I know how touchy they are. (*Moves toward the closet*) Don't forget. Two o'clock matinee, tomorrow.

MARGO   Thanks. Good night.

(*She goes out and pauses, thoughtfully.* EVE *hangs up* MARGO'*s dress and takes her own coat from the closet*)

DUANE (*After a pause*)   Anything wrong?

MARGO (*Shaking it off*)   No, no, nothing.

(They leave, and a moment later HOWARD *comes into the dressing room)*

HOWARD Eve.

EVE Oh, Mr. Benedict, I think you can just catch Miss Channing.

HOWARD I've been hanging around to catch *you,* and thank you for taking my side.

EVE I wouldn't have said it if I hadn't meant it.

HOWARD Join me for a drink?

EVE Well . . .

HOWARD I must toast the new Prime Minister.

EVE What?

HOWARD The power behind Queen Margo.

EVE *(With a little laugh)* I don't know what you're talking about.

HOWARD I think you do. You're a very interesting girl. Come on. Joe Allen's. Just down the block. The gypsies go there after their shows.

*(*HOWARD *helps* EVE *into her coat. The* GYPSIES—*boy and girl dancers—enter as the dressing-room set is being removed)*

GYPSIES (*Singing another version of "Backstage Babble"*)
Ba ba da, ba ba da,
Ba ba da, ba ba da,
Tryout for summer stock . . .

EVE   Gypsies?

HOWARD   Gypsy, my dear, is the name dancers affectionately give themselves as they go camping from show to
show.

GYPSIES (*Setting up tables*)
Ba da ba, da ba da,
And then I said to him . . .

PIANO PLAYER (*At a piano being moved into place for the
next scene*)   Hi, Mr. Benedict! How's the new musical
in Philly?

HOWARD   Lousy book, lousy score. Naturally everyone is
blaming the costumes.

GYPSIES
Ba ba da, résumé,
Ba ba da, ba ba da,
Agents are all ba da . . .

(HOWARD *motions* EVE *to an empty table. She sits,
and he is about to, but he is stopped by a gypsy girl
seated at the next table who sticks her leg out and
blocks his path for the moment*)

GYPSY GIRL (*Enthusiastically*)   My ankle's okay. I'm back
in the show.

HOWARD *(Dismissing her)*   Oh! Terrific.

(He joins EVE *and sits at the table)*

GYPSIES
Ba ba da, ba da, ba da ba,
Ba ba da, ba da . . .

(They repeat the refrain, to a fade-out finish)

SCENE SIX

There has been no break in the action, but the set has now completely changed, and the scene is Joe Allen's, a bar and restaurant on West 46th Street in New York. The GYPSIES—*dancers and singers, patrons of Joe Allen's—have carried in the tables and chairs, the tables covered with bright red-checkered tablecloths.*

There are three large window arches and a door arch. The decor is of simulated red brick. A bar folds out from behind and to the right of the unit as it comes into position. A set of double doors swings on and locks into place.

The red-brick wall on the left is covered with pictures and with framed signs of Broadway shows. At the top of the wall are two blackboard menus, the daily specials prominent in chalk.

Waiters in shirt-sleeves are dashing between the kitchen door and the bar.

EVE   You have so many friends.

HOWARD   Friends! They're either in one of my shows or trying to get in.

(STAN HARDING, *a columnist, approaches their table*)

STAN (*Joining them, speaking over* HOWARD's *shoulder*) Howard!

46

HOWARD (*Turning*) Oh, it's you, Stan. Eve, this is Stan Harding. I'm sure you read his nitwit chatter column religiously. Eve Harrington.

STAN Hello.

HOWARD This guy specializes in using all the old Leonard Lyons and Earl Wilson rejects. Miss Harrington is Margo's secretary.

STAN (*Moving to* EVE's *right*) Ah . . . If you want to do your boss a favor, tell Her Highness that a certain columnist thinks just once she ought to return his phone calls. Every other biggie does.

EVE Don't blame her, she's an extraordinary woman. That must have been a terrible oversight on *my* part. It won't happen again.

STAN Good quality, loyalty. Nice girl, Howard. See you.

(*He moves to his own table. A waiter rushes by, before* HOWARD *can hail him*)

HOWARD That *was* our waiter who just flew by, wasn't it?

(*A young woman across the room laughs*)

EVE Oh, there's Miss Channing's understudy.

HOWARD (*Looking*) Oh, yes.

EVE (*As if to herself*) Why does she keep doing it?

HOWARD Doing what?

47

EVE (*Casually*) You know, Bert is a very conscientious stage manager. He noticed that she has been standing in the wings right where Miss Channing can see her, mimicking everything she does. He's spoken to her a dozen times, but he's beginning to lose patience.

HOWARD (*With a sigh*) Here we go again, looking for an understudy. Say, Karen told me *you* know every line of the play.

EVE (*Glowing*) Every line, every move! I've watched it so many times, and Miss Channing still makes me laugh and cry every time!

HOWARD Karen even suggested you if we should need a new understudy.

EVE Me?

(BONNIE, *one of the* GYPSIES, *enters and joins a nearby table*)

HOWARD Would you be interested in reading for it?

EVE I don't think so. I'm happy behind the scenes or out in the audience.

HOWARD You're a pretty cool character. There are kids in this place who'd *kill* for a chance like this! Danny!

DANNY (*A* GYPSY *at another table*) Yes, Mr. Benedict.

HOWARD Eve Harrington, Danny Burns.

48

EVE   How do you do.

HOWARD   Danny, if you were starving and had to sell something, which would you choose . . . your dancing shoes or your mother?

DANNY   My mother!

EVE   You really love what you're doing. You're very lucky.

GYPSY GIRL   Oh, we're *very* lucky.

BONNIE *(Rising)*   Sure. Do you know we make a hundred and sixty-four dollars and fifty cents a week?

DANNY   Every week we work, that is.

CAROL *(A GYPSY)*   And by statistics, we work an average of fourteen weeks a year.

BONNIE   So minus acting classes, singing and dancing lessons . . .

(*This as well as the following dialogue is underscored by the PIANO PLAYER*)

DANNY   Equity dues . . .

CAROL   Social security tax . . .

GYPSY GIRL   And cat food . . .

BONNIE   Leaves about twelve dollars and fifteen cents take-home pay. And it's so simple. You only have to study for ten years, and if you're lucky your career can last another ten . . . *(She does a step, and her knee hits the floor)* Unless you happen to smash your kneecap! But then you can always make eccentric jewelry at home and sell it to your friends . . . But it's all worth it—and why?

EVE   Why?

GYPSIES *(Ad-libbing)*   You tell 'em . . .

> *(BONNIE looks around. They all look puzzled. She gets an idea, does a warm-up, and goes over to HOWARD and EVE's table, where she whips off the tablecloth without disturbing a thing. EVE spontaneously applauds. BONNIE nods at her)*

BONNIE *(She sings "Applause" and is joined by the GYPSIES)*

What is it that we're living for?
Applause, applause.
Nothing I know
Brings on the glow
Like sweet applause.

You're thinking you're through,
That nobody cares,
Then suddenly you
Hear it . . . starting . . .

And somehow you're in charge again,
And it's a ball!
Trumpets all sing,
Life seems to swing,
And you're the king
Of it all, 'cause . . .

You've had a taste of

The sound that says love,
Applause,
Applause,
Applause!

MALE GYPSY

When I was eight
I was in a school play,
I'll never forget it,
I had one line to say!
My big moment came,
I said, "What, ho, the prince!"
My sister applauded,
I've been hooked ever since!

BONNIE

It's better than pot!
It's better than booze!
A shot of applause
Will stamp out the blues.
You work till you're dead,
It ain't for the bread,
Call me out of my head!

Your bank account's bare,
Your cat has the flu,
You're losing your hair,
Then you . . . hear it . . .

> (At this point the GYPSIES begin to clap, starting
> with a low, distant sound, working their way up
> to a thunderous roar of applause)

ALL

That happy sound rolls over you,
And just like that,

Everything's bright,
This is the night,
Love hits you right where
You're at, 'cause . . .

You've had a taste of
The sound that says love,
Applause,
Applause,
There's wondr'ous applause,
Thund'rous applause,
Beautiful, soaring,
Magnificent, roaring!
It's better than pot!
It's better than booze!
A shot of applause
Will stamp out the blues.
Whatever you do you do better because
You're doing it to the beat of applause.
And nothing can beat the beat of applause.
When you hear it . . .

(*Under* BONNIE'*s direction, the* GYPSIES *put together
a little stage made up of tables. Some pull up chairs
and act as audience, while others go behind the arch-
ways, which become entrances to the improvised
stage. They put on a rousing, satirical show, starting
with quick take-offs of show-stopping moments in the
annals of musical comedy history, ranging from a
Rose-Marie duet à la Jeannette MacDonald/Nelson
Eddy, through* Hello, Dolly! Fiddler on the Roof,
Cabaret, West Side Story, *all using the word "applause" somewhere in the lyric, and finally winding
up with a competition between three* GYPSIES *trying*

to do a wholesome rendition of Oklahoma, *while, to
their horror, three others are yelling "Oh! Calcutta!"
and stripping down to their bare bottoms. The finale
is pure vaudeville; tap dancers, ballet dancers, con-
tortionists, baton-twirlers, jugglers, roller skaters, etc.,
all doing their individual routines at the same time,
and ending with* BONNIE *popping up out of a huge
serving dish. It is an all-out display of show-biz corn
that begs the audience for that "big hand." Stepping
forward at the end, with arms outstretched, they join
together to sing)*

ALL

Why do we work our asses off?
What is it for?
Cares disappear
Soon as you hear
That happy audience roar, 'cause
You've had a taste of
The sound that says love
Applause!
Applause!
Applause!

(The GYPSIES *excitedly receive their applause from
the theater audience, then form a parade, led across
by the flag-twirler. During this, the set is being
struck behind them)*

ALL

Wherever you are it's always the same
Whenever applause is calling your name,
No matter what kind,
Never mind,
You don't care

As long as it's there . . .
And somehow you're in charge again,
And it's a ball.
Trumpets all sing,
Life seems to swing,
And you're the king
Of it all, 'cause
You've had a taste of
The sound that says love,
Applause!
Applause!
Applause!

(BONNIE *has led* HOWARD *and* EVE *over to watch the parade, and now pulls* EVE *in to dance with her on the last few bars. The* GYPSIES *carry off what remains of the set, and* HOWARD *and* EVE *wave good-bye to them, and exit together)*

The scene is Margo's bedroom later that night. This set moves on from the right and is dominated by a large brass-framed bed. There is a door to the right of the stage, and next to it a hat rack. A yellow lamp with a purple shade sits on a table at the right side of the bed. On the left is an elephant-based table with a clock and a telephone.

A second door, upstage from the entrance door, leads to the bathroom. To its left is a bookcase with an oval mirror above. On the bureau is a blue vase filled with white and yellow roses.

On the other side of the stage, the left, is a bay window with three windows. The seats below are covered with pink cushions. Left of the seats is a desk which matches the bureau, and a chair pushed underneath. Next to one of the table legs on the left is a glass figure of a greyhound. The floor is covered with a plush white rug, and between the bed and the desk is a large pile of pillows of various colors.

The room is quite dark. MARGO *is alseep as the phone rings. She stirs. It rings again, and she fumbles for the light, switches it on, then picks up the phone.*

MARGO *(Sleepily)* H'lo.

OPERATOR'S VOICE We're ready with your call to Rome.

MARGO Call? What call? *(She squints at her clock)* It's three A.M.

OPERATOR'S VOICE   Is this Templeton 0-8842? Miss Margo Channing?

MARGO   I think so . . .

OPERATOR'S VOICE   We're ready with the call you placed to Mr. William Sampson for eight A.M. Rome time.

MARGO   *I* placed?

ITALIAN OPERATOR'S VOICE   Pronto! . . . Meester Sampson . . . go ahead!

> (BILL *appears to the left of the stage, holding a phone*)

BILL   Margo!

MARGO   Bill!

BILL   You stayed up so late just to talk to me!

MARGO *(Fuzzily)*   Yeah . . .

BILL   I'm not mad you're calling me on the set, but come on, say it . . . it's twelve thousand dollars a minute . . .

MARGO *(Rising)*   Well, sure . . . I love you.

BILL   We know all that . . . get to the point.

MARGO   Huh?

BILL *(laughing)*   Come on, Margo. I'll be a year older before you get to it.

(MARGO *gets out of the bed, suddenly wide awake*)

MARGO (*Guiltily*) Bill, it's your birthday—

BILL And you remembered . . . you sweet thing.

MARGO Happy Birthday, darling.

BILL Thank you.

MARGO (*Sinks to the pillows, lying on her back. The audience sees her face upside-down*) Oh, Bill, without you I'm beginning to climb walls . . . turning into a genuine crazy lady. I threatened Benedict with a breakdown if he didn't let me go to Rome for a week. Didn't work . . .

BILL Aw, baby, I feel the same way . . . Listen, till I get back, use up your energy on things like hating Emerson for upstaging you and—

MARGO Hey, how'd you know that?

BILL Eve wrote me. She hasn't missed a week since I left. Keeps me filled in on all the backstage goings-on . . . everything you've been up to. You probably tell her what to write.

MARGO (*Sits up*) Oh, sure.

BILL I sent her a list of my addresses on location for the next couple of weeks, so if you want to get in touch with me, check with Eve.

MARGO (*Stands up*) Right.

BILL Do you love me?

MARGO I'll check with Eve. I mean—of course I do.

BILL (*Singing*)

> Hey, flash your famous smile . . .
> Are you smiling?
>> The one that gets 'em all,
>> Think how it's gonna be . . .
> *Arriverderci, cara mia.*

MARGO Good-bye Bill . . .

> (*They both hang up*)

BILL

> Think how it's gonna be
> When we're together again.

> (*The light blacks out on him.* MARGO *paces around her room desperately*)

MARGO'S VOICE (*On tape, singing "Hurry Back"*)

> Hurry back,
> Hurry back,
> It's no life at all
> When you're not here to hold me.

> Hurry back,
> Hurry back,
> What's the point of doing crazy things

When you're not here to scold me?
Honey . . .

(Walks over to the desk)

MARGO *(Singing aloud, as her taped voice fades)*

Honey,
Hurry back,
Hurry back,
When I get you here
I'll give you so much love
You'll never leave me,
Believe me,
Hurry back.

(Goes over to the pillows and sinks down)

Come back home,
I'm so lonely.
There's so much to say
And so much love to make up.

Hurry back,
Hurry back,
I'll just die unless I see your face
Beside me when I wake up.

(Pulls herself up)

Honey . . .

Hurry back,
Make it fast,
Hurry back,
I can't last . . .
Hurry back.

(She sinks back on the pile of pillows on the floor. The lights go down. After a few moments they come on again. It is morning. MARGO is in bed. EVE knocks, enters, carrying a tray, crosses to the desk, and puts the tray down)

EVE *(Businesslike)* 'Morning. Nothing fascinating in the mail.

MARGO *(Groggily)* 'Morning.

EVE *(Handing a glass of orange juice to MARGO)* Duane's here. He wants to pick up your fall . . .

MARGO Sure.
 (DUANE enters)

DUANE Hi, Duchess.

MARGO Hi, Duane. Want some coffee?

DUANE Thanks.

(He goes to the desk to help himself. EVE walks back to the desk to get some bills in the drawer)

EVE Hope you had a good night's sleep. I'll get started on the bills. Oh, and I've made up a list of tax deductions you haven't been taking.

MARGO *(Faintly annoyed)* You think of everything.

EVE *(Starts to leave)* That's my job.

MARGO Eve, by any chance, did you place a call from me to Bill, eight A.M. Rome time?

EVE *(Stops)* Oh, I forgot to tell you! That meeting in the dressing room knocked it out of my head completely.

MARGO Don't worry about it. It was very thoughtful of you.

EVE Mr. Sampson's birthday! I knew you'd never forgive me if I forgot that. *(Starts to exit)* As a matter of fact, I sent him a cable myself.

(She exits. MARGO *and* DUANE *exchange a look)*

DUANE I saw her at Joe Allen's last night. She was table-for-twoing it with everybody's favorite producer.

MARGO Out with Howard? How extraordinary. *(The phone rings. She picks it up)* Hello? . . . Rome? *(Stands up, grabs* DUANE'S *hand, worried)* Yes, yes, go ahead! Bill! Anything wrong? . . . *No! Two weeks!* . . . You bet you'll get a coming home party—pin-the-tail-on-the-donkey, paper hats . . . *(Turns* DUANE *around)* an orgy! . . . Right. Love you! *(She hangs up, ecstatic, and kicks a cushion.* DUANE *catches it)* Duane! Two weeks! He's coming home in two weeks! I told him how desperate I was; now they're letting him bring the film and cut it here! And all because Eve placed that call! *(*DUANE *drops the cushion)* You don't like her, do you? *(*DUANE *rolls his eyes heavenward in disgust)* But Duane, she's marvelous! She thinks only of me.

DUANE *(Going over to the bed)* Let's say she thinks only *about* you. Studying you. The way you walk, the way you talk, the way you dress. *(He sings in a falsetto voice, imitating* EVE*)*

"The best night of my life . . ."

MARGO (*Laughing and giving* DUANE *a push so he falls on the bed*) How do I look? I've got to look new! Different! Misty! Feminine! *Italian!* Duane, how do you say "Welcome home, Bill" in Italian?

DUANE I don't know. See what happens if you try *"Vesti la giubba,* Bill!"

MARGO Of course! *Vesti la giubba,* Bill!

(*Laughing, she and* DUANE *start dancing a wild tarantella, which they continue as they move off with the bedroom set while the scene changes*)

The scene is Margo's living room, two weeks later. The bedroom set moves off to the right, and two waiters enter from the left, carrying a large banner reading "Vesti la Giubba, Bill." They are followed in by KAREN, *in evening dress, who has a number of name-game signs over her shoulder and a pencil holder in her hand.* BUZZ, *in black tie, enters behind* KAREN)

KAREN (*Looking at the banner*)   What does that mean?

BUZZ (*Laughing confidently, then breaking off*)   What does that mean? . . . I don't know. Isn't this an anti-climax? Bill's been home two days already.

KAREN   She promised him a party . . . (*The waiters go behind the sofa, where they place the banner. The omelet man, Rudy, crosses behind* KAREN, *pushing his cart.* KAREN *motions him to a position on the right. A bartender enters and walks up to the bar. On the terrace are three* MUSICIANS, *noisily setting up their instruments and tuning them. The bar has been set with several whiskey bottles and extra glasses. On the corner of the terrace is a candelabra, rigged so that the candles will appear to burn down to denote the passage of time. The* MUSICIANS *blare loudly.* KAREN *moves toward the sofa*) Hey, fellas! Cut! Cut! (*They stop*) Why don't you go to the kitchen and stuff yourselves until the guests start piling in? (*The*

MUSICIANS *start collecting themselves, muttering hip phrases at her, like "Dig it baby," and exit.* KAREN *puts the pencil holder on the left arm of the sofa*) I've never seen Margo so nervous. You'd think it was her first prom. She's changing her outfit for the fourth time.

BUZZ And she's had a martini for each change.

KAREN Oh, no! (EVE *enters, wearing the dress* MARGO *wore to the village bar on opening night. She looks radiant and shapely, suddenly a woman*) Oh, Eve, don't you look smashing.

(BUZZ *stares at* EVE)

EVE (*Moving to the center of the stage and turning around to flair the skirt*) Do I? Miss Channing gave it to me. It just needed a little alteration. You're sure I don't look foolish in it?

KAREN I should look so foolish. Buzz, look at Eve.

BUZZ You don't have to tell me. I'm looking.

KAREN (*To* EVE) Now I'm really convinced. You know, that idea we talked about? Your reading for the understudy? You've *got* to.

EVE Oh, no, it was a silly idea.

BUZZ What do you mean? Karen's got good instincts. Try for it.

EVE Well, we'll see.

KAREN *(Hanging one of the signs around* EVE's *neck)* Here, put this on. No, you mustn't look.

EVE What is it?

BUZZ It's a game. Bill's hooked on them.

KAREN There's a famous name on it. Everyone gets one as he comes in the door. You have to guess who you are by the way people talk to you, and *you* talk to them the way you would if they really were those people. You'll catch on.

BUZZ *(Indicating the signs)* C'mon Karen, let's put these out in the hall.

> *(*BUZZ *and* KAREN *exit.* EVE *turns, and on her back is the sign "Freud." She sits on the couch and accidentally knocks the pencil holder off the arm. She bends over the back to reach it.* BILL *enters, wearing a sign on his back, "Greta Garbo," and sees just* EVE's *bottom and legs, and her back with the sign on it. Mistaking her for* MARGO, *because of the dress, he pats her lightly on the bottom)*

BILL Your subconscious is showing, my darling!

> *(*EVE *jumps up, startled.* BILL *jumps back, embarrassed)*

EVE Oh, Bill . . . uh . . . Mr. Sampson!

BILL Good God, I thought you were . . .

(He points at what she's wearing. They both talk at once)

EVE   Miss Channing gave me this—

BILL   Eve . . . forgive me . . . I—*(They both break off, look at each other, and laugh)* Where *is* she?

EVE   She's dressing . . . a little behind schedule. Everyone will be here in a minute. *(BILL starts up the steps to the bedroom. EVE detains him by speaking)* Uh . . . what was that about my subconscious?

BILL   Oh. *(Instantly drawn into the game and coming back down toward her, by the sofa)* Uh . . . I would say you have a giant brain, my good man, but a smallish beard.

EVE   William Shakespeare!

BILL   *(Heavily Teutonic)*   Nein!

EVE   *Nein.* Uh . . . Einstein? No, he only had that mustache. Let me see who you are. *(She looks at his sign and goes around the sofa. He sits on the right arm)* Oh. *(She sits in the swivel chair. With a terrible Swedish accent)* I'm surprised you came to the party. I thought you vould vant to be alone.

BILL   *(Laughing and pulling his sign around)*   You're not supposed to make it so easy. I'm Garbo, who else?

EVE   I guess I'm not very good at games.

BILL   Of course you are. Now you're going to guess who you are if it takes all night. *(He takes her by the hands and seats her on the couch. He circles the sofa behind her. In a Viennese accent)* Imagine my running into you here. Are you still ze pride of Vienna?

EVE   Did Johann Strauss have a beard?

BILL   *Nein! Nein! (Impulsively takes the pillow and puts it in her lap, then lies with his head on it and his thumb in his mouth)* I vill simply have to lie down on zis couch und tell you all about it. You zee, ven I vas a little boy, my muzzer . . .

EVE   You mean if you tell me your dreams, I could maybe help you?

BILL   *(Encouragingly)*   Aha! Aha!

EVE   I should have guessed it right away. Sigmund Freud!

BILL   No, Adolf Hitler! *(They both burst out laughing, BILL still with his head in her lap. At this point MARGO enters from the bedroom and takes in the scene. BILL, seeing her, gets up)* Margo!

EVE   *(Getting up and turning to MARGO)*   Oh, Miss Channing, we were just playing the game.

MARGO   *(Menacingly flat)*   One of the oldest.

BILL   *(Taking off the sign and putting it on the coffee table)* The kid, here, couldn't guess she was Freud till I—

MARGO   I wonder if the kid would mind checking to see why Rudy, the omelet man, isn't here.

EVE   I'd be glad to.

MARGO Thank you so much. And just remember as you go through life that for every whole omelet there are two broken eggs.
(EVE *exits*)

BILL *(With enthusiasm, lovingly)* Margo, this looks like a party for a man who loves games, omelets, dancing —and crazy, beautiful stars. He's a pretty lucky guy. Thank you, my darling.

MARGO *(Going up to the bar, moving away from him as he comes toward her)* I didn't even know you were here.

BILL *(Casually)* I ran into Eve on my way up, and she said you were dressing.

MARGO *(Going down the steps, avoiding him)* That never stopped you before.

BILL Well, we started playing your sign game . . . the kid hasn't been around to these parties much . . .

MARGO True. She's so innocent, so unspoiled.

BILL Well, those are pretty rare qualities these days.

MARGO She's a girl of so many rare qualities. So you've been telling me these last two days—warm, devoted, so young and fair.

BILL *(With great control)* The kid's okay. Now darling—

MARGO *(Cutting in)* Stop calling her a kid! Since you've been back, you two have had *so* much to talk over—in corners, here, at the theater, God knows where else . . .

BILL *(Moving toward her)* Margo, you're hallucinating!

MARGO *(Moving back)* So many things to chew over. Your trying to make films, her trying to make you . . .

BILL *(Bursting out)* What the hell are you talking about?

MARGO I'm talking about the departments of my life I want exclusively to myself—*you,* in particular! Hands off! No trespassing! Especially from the "warm," the "devoted," the "young," the "fair."

(MARGO *sits on the left side of the sofa)*

BILL *(After a tense pause)* I suppose this is my cue to grab you in my arms and drown your silly doubts in an ocean of wet kisses, but I can't! I'm too damn mad!

MARGO Guilty!

BILL *(Moving to the right side of the sofa and around back)* No, *mad!* I turned a movie studio upside down to get back here to you. I missed you. I wanted you so much. But to come back to the same old fruit stand—this age obsession of yours . . . *(She gets up and goes to the omelet cart. He follows, but then turns away)* And now this ridiculous attempt to whip yourself up into a jealous froth because I spend ten minutes with a stage-struck kid who worships you. It shows a paranoiac insecurity you ought to be ashamed of!

MARGO Paranoiac. A term you picked up, no doubt, from the vivacious Dr. Freud!

(During this exchange, EVE has entered and is behind MARGO)

EVE *(Low-voiced, discreetly)* Excuse me, Miss Channing, the omelet man will be right in, the guests should be arriving, and I thought you might like another martini.

(She hands MARGO a martini, takes her glass, and goes up to the bar)

MARGO Isn't she a treasure? . . . I think I'll bury her! *(The MUSICIANS come back in. BILL goes to the sofa)* Ah, boys, music . . . music . . . music! *(Some GUESTS start arriving including HOWARD, KAREN, and BUZZ. The GUESTS are dressed in the high styles of the moment, ranging from the quietly chic to the wildly bizarre. Each one has a sign on his back with a famous name on it)* Ah, my guests! All my little friends from Madame Tussaud's Wax Works.

HOWARD Hello, Margo!

MARGO Ah! Howard. You all know the guest of honor— Greta Garbo!

(She presents BILL)

KAREN Margo, cut it out.

MARGO *(As HOWARD moves to the center of the stage, she pulls his sign to the front; it reads "Al Capone")* Oh, Al Capone! Oh, Eve—Eve, you two must meet. You have so much in common.

(She turns and greets PETER)

PETER   How are you, Margo?

MARGO   Don't ask. (*She moves to another guest, Bob, at the omelet table*) And Bill! Look who's here! The Great Lover—Rudolf Valentino! You could teach him a thing or two. Ha, ha, ha.

(*She laughs;* BILL *imitates her laugh*)

HOWARD (*Taking off his sign and handing it to* EVE)   Well, there goes *that* game.

MARGO   Yes, Howard, but we can all still play the game of life—where some win, some lose, some cheat, some lie!

BUZZ (*Joining* KAREN *on the sofa*)   I can smell the sulphur in the air. What's going on?

MARGO (*Fairly tight by now. On the terrace, with her back to the audience*)   Step up, step up, folks. Continuous performance! Thrills, spills, chills! Watch the little lady do a back bend and pick up her heart with her teeth! Hurry, hurry, hurry!

KAREN (*Sitting on the sofa*)   Margo, is this the beginning or the end of something?
    (MARGO *is standing near the bass fiddle*)

MARGO   Fasten your seat belts . . . (*She plucks a bass-fiddle string, and there is a noisy twang. All eyes are on her*) It's going to be a bumpy night!

(*She goes up to the bar.* BUZZ, KAREN, HOWARD, BILL, *and* DUANE *sing "Fasten Your Seat Belts"*)

BUZZ

  Fasten your seat belts,
  It's gonna be a bumpy night,
   (Makes a raspy S.O.S. sound)
  Eh eh eh eh.

  Batten the hatches,
  We're gonna have a funsy flight!
  Eh eh eh eh.

KAREN *(Joining* BUZZ*)*

  She's laughing a bit too loudly,
  That's how the last one began . . .

HOWARD *(Meeting* BILL *in the center of the stage)*

  I figure she's two drinks from the spot
  Where you-know-what
  Hits the fan!

  (Several new GUESTS *enter)*

BILL *and* HOWARD *(To two* GUESTS*)*
  Don't take off your coat,
  You came the wrong night.
  Get out while you can,
  Mother is uptight!

KAREN, BUZZ, HOWARD, BILL, and DUANE
  Fasten your seat belts,
  It's gonna be, eh eh eh eh eh eh,
  A bumpy night!

BUZZ Let's get out of here.

KAREN We can't. It's Bill's party.

BUZZ Best party since the St. Valentine's Day Massacre.

(BILL *and* HOWARD *sit on the sofa*)

KAREN, BUZZ, HOWARD, BILL, and DUANE
    Fasten your seat belts,
    Say all your prayers and hold on tight,
    Drink and be merry,
    For the *Titanic* sails tonight,
    All aboard,
    It will be
    A bumpy night!

(KAREN *sits on the bench;* BUZZ *sits on the arm.* EVE
*walks over to them, and the music continues to play
in the background while they speak*)

EVE *(Unhappily)* I'm so puzzled. What did I do to
offend Miss Channing?

BUZZ It's beyond me.

KAREN You've done nothing but wonders for Margo.

MARGO *(Joining the group in time to hear to* KAREN's *last
line)* My dear, would you perform another of your wonders and bring me one of *my* hometown toddies—a double
martini? And don't put your pretty little thumb in it, I
don't want to die of sugar poisoning.

*(EVE goes to a waiter standing near the steps, gets a
martini and hands it to MARGO)*

KAREN, BUZZ, HOWARD, BILL, and DUANE
Fasten your seat belts,
It's gonna be a bumpy night. Eh eh eh eh.
Margo in action,
Critics have called an awesome sight!
Eh eh eh eh.

*(The music continues in the background as EVE calls
HOWARD aside)*

HOWARD   Don't worry about Margo. These lady stars—
they suffer and suffer, but we're the ones that wind up
with the ulcers. Has Margo Channing ever been sick?
Which reminds me, Bert did fire the understudy. Too
bad it's of no interest to you.

EVE   I tell you what. You set up your auditions, and that
day . . . well, maybe, just for the hell of it—

*(MARGO has wandered up near them, with her back
to the audience, and catching EVE's last words, she
wheels around)*

MARGO   Oh! "The hell of it"! Eve, such language! You go
straight to your room—the one in Madison, Wisconsin!

*(At this point a girl enters, wearing a revealing,
black-beaded costume. She is followed by BILL, a
girl in an East Indian outfit, DUANE, and a girl in a
slave costume. They move toward MARGO)*

BILL
I've seen the Taj Mahal at dawn,

DUANE
The Hanging Gardens of Babylon,

BILL and DUANE (*With oriental head movements*)
But nothing compares with Miss Channing
When she's on,

BUZZ and KAREN
And she's on!

HOWARD
Yeah, she's on!

BILL
Oh, she's on!

ALL
And she's on,
Yeah, she's on!

> (*A dance number follows, with* MARGO, *a girl carrying a feather boa, and the girl in the beaded costume. There is stripper music, and the boa is utilized in the dance.* MARGO *executes some deft bumps and grinds and stripper walks, which convey a to-hell-with-you attitude to* BILL)

It's going to be a bumpy night!

MARGO
Here's a bump here,
There's a bump there,

GIRL WITH FEATHER BOA
> Here's a bump,

GIRL IN BEADED COSTUME
> There's a bump,

MARGO
> Everywhere a bump bump,
> Turbulence ahead,
> Turbulence behind,
> Ready, girls?

> *(Turns to the girl in the beaded costume)*

> Silly dress!

> *(To a girl well-endowed)*

> Silicone!

> *(To a girl in a maternity dress)*

> Single girl!

> *(MARGO sees EVE standing in front of the omelet cart)*

Eve!

> *(Everybody freezes. The music stops. MARGO circles in front of EVE)* You do look lovely in that dress. So smart! You had your eye on it from the beginning. I'm glad I gave it to you. Anything else you have your eye on? *(EVE backs away from MARGO, not quite sure of MARGO's intent. MARGO then grabs EVE, and singing her own accompaniment of "Who's That Girl," does a few jitterbug steps with her as she did that first night EVE came along. MARGO spins EVE out and she bumps against BILL,*

coming toward them. The whole room is watching tensely. After a moment of silence) You may all resume breathing. *(She circles around the bench and walks up to the bar)* On to the next game . . . Why don't you all choose up sides and go home!

GUESTS

    Thanks for the party!
    Wow! What a blast!
    Pick up the pieces,
    Let's get out fast,
    Get your coat,
    Where's the door?
    Man, it's been, eh eh eh eh eh,
    A bumpy night, eh eh eh eh eh,
    A bumpy night . . .

    (The GUESTS *slip out as the music diminuendoes and the lights dim . . . The candles burn down and the room takes on an after-the-party view: used plates, cups, napkins, etc., are scattered here and there. At a bench which was placed earlier close to the omelet cart are* EVE, BILL, HOWARD, BUZZ, *and* KAREN*)*

BILL   Is it dawn yet? I can't believe it, but I've got to be in that cutting room at eight A.M.

    *(*MARGO *weaves over to them, carrying a saxophone. She blows it.* EVE *jumps to her feet)*

MARGO *(Moving between* BILL *and* EVE*)* Don't get up. You needn't act as if I were the Queen Mother.

77

EVE   I'm sorry, I—
(EVE *runs out the door*)

BILL   Outside of a beehive, I wouldn't consider your behavior either queenly or motherly.

(MARGO *blows on the sax again*)

KAREN   Really, Margo, it's time you realized that what's attractive on stage is not necessarily attractive off.

MARGO   I haven't your unfailing good taste. I wish I had gone to "Radcliffee," too, but father needed my help at the fish market.

BILL *(Wearily)*   Cut it out!

MARGO   This is my house, not a theater. You're a guest here, not a direct*awr*!

BUZZ   Then stop being a star.

HOWARD   And stop treating your friends as your supporting cast.

MARGO   Supporting! That's a joke. All of you . . . living off *my* hide! *My* charisma! *(She bursts into song and dance to "La Cucaracha."* BILL, BUZZ, HOWARD *and* KAREN *leave)*
    La-ca-ca-risma!
    La-ca-ca-risma!
    Ca-ca-ca-ca-la-la-la!

(*She hands the omelet man the saxophone*)

Here, fry this!

(She gets up on the bench. In her deepest voice)
Now hear this . . . hear this. This is your captain speaking!

(Singing drunkenly)

Fasten your seat belts,
It's really been a bumpy night,
I've got a secret,
I think I'm just a wee bit tight . . .

(This breaks her up, and giggling, she collapses. A waiter catches her and puts her behind the bench)

Everybody bail out! Ooh, look at the star . . . The star is on her ass. Her parachute wouldn't open. Eve must have packed it!

(With a little laugh, she lets her head fall forward on the bench)

DUANE *(Moving from the bar to the terrace, surveying the wreckage of the room)* Nothing will ever grow here again.

MARGO *(Looking up)* Ah, the party's thinning out . . . down to my closest friends.

DUANE *(Walking over to MARGO, pulling her up and moving toward the swivel chair)* No, your closest friends have all left. Personally, I don't blame them. You were the worst. Bill said he'd call you tomorrow.

MARGO Was he mad?

DUANE No, just hurt.

MARGO I know that martyred look. Like St. Sebastian after the arrows hit. (DUANE *helps her into the swivel chair. She keeps swiveling about*) I'll call *him* . . . Maybe I *won't* . . . Maybe I will. I'm sorry I behaved badly . . . No, I'm *not!* My friends should know that's not the real me! . . . Yes, it *is.* I'm the worst. (*Brightening up*) Not always! Sometimes I'm adorable! (*Gets up and goes up the steps, shouting defiantly against the music of* "But Alive")

I'm a thousand diff'rent people,
Ev'ry single one is real.
I've a million diff'rent feelings,
Okay, but at least I feel,
At least I feel,
I *feel* . . .

(*As the set moves up and off with* MARGO *on it, her voice can still be heard, overlapping with* EVE's *voice as the backstage set comes on*)

The scene takes place backstage, several days later. The set is the side view of a bare stage, as if looking from the left wings. On the right is the proscenium. EVE *is auditioning, facing into the right wings.* BERT, *holding a script, is reading with her.*

There are footlights upstage and to the right. Against the back wall is a stage manager's desk, with a clipboard hanging on the side and various papers atop. A tormentor boom with five lights is next to the desk.

There is a sliding stage door right of center. It closes from left to right and has a counterweight. To the left of the door are a fire extinguisher, a trunk with a chair upside down on top, an old chair left of the trunk, a large mirror, and then a spiral staircase, used from time to time during the show. It leads to a flyfloor approximately ten feet above the stage level, and ropes tied around pins are visible. The flyfloor is also used, so it must be strongly constructed.

The stage left wall is the stage right wall of MARGO's *dressing-room set in its offstage storage position. A door is in the center of the wall. From the left has come a red chaise, followed by a gilded birdcage, a fern in a gold wicker basket, and an old dressing screen. The chaise stops left of center, the three trailing objects two feet behind.* EVE's *voice is heard before the lights are fully up.*

EVE's VOICE I feel . . . I feel . . . fed up with being on display! An ornament! A Tiffany glass bottle with nothing inside. There *is* something inside!

(The lights go up as she is finishing. She is wearing a short, clinging dress, and for the first time she appears provocatively sexy)

BERT *(Also reading from a script)*   What do you want?

EVE   Nothing from you. I found someone who held that bottle up to the light, rubbed it in the right places, said some delicious magic words, and out popped the genie . . . me! And I'm never going back in! I like it out here! *(Applause is heard, and* BUZZ, KAREN, HOWARD, *and* BILL *come out onto the stage.* BERT *congratulates* EVE *affectionately, then moves to the desk as the others join her. A stage hand enters, goes up the spiral staircase to the flyfloor, and lowers the overhead work light)*

BUZZ *(Carried away, crossing to* EVE*)*   Eve . . . I didn't want you to stop!

EVE   Oh, Mr. Richards!

BUZZ   It was like hearing my play for the first time . . . Please don't misunderstand me. Margo acts the part marvelously . . . but hearing it read by someone who's *really* . . . the youth, the vitality . . . my words came alive!

KAREN *(Glowing)*   I'm supposed to butt out, but I just can't. I feel so proud.

EVE   Oh, thank you, Karen.

BILL *(Crossing to* EVE *and shaking her hand)*   That was

a helluva first reading. After watching Margo all these months, it wasn't an imitation—you made it your own. I'm very impressed.

EVE   Oh, Mr. Sampson, I was so nervous, mainly because of you. By now we're almost friends, but *you*—I hardly know you at all. (*Tremulous giggle*) I was petrified!

HOWARD   Bert! How many waiting to read?

BERT (*At the desk*)   Five more.

HOWARD   No point in wasting their time. Miss Harrington's got the job. Thank them nicely and send them home.

BERT   Yes, sir!

HOWARD   Eve, welcome to the theater.

BUZZ   Welcome aboard!

(MARGO *enters through the stage door*)

MARGO   Who's welcoming who to what?

ALL (*Ad-libbing*)   Hello, Margo!

BILL   Margo, it's after three.

MARGO   Well?

BILL   The auditions began at two.

MARGO (*Moving over to the chaise*)   Well, how many stars turn up for these goddamn readings at all. I had a luncheon interview in connection with this very play we are all living on, and it ran late. I'm truly sorry. *(She takes off her coat)* Oh, come on, let's not stay mad at each other because of the other night. Now, shall we begin?

BUZZ   It's over.

MARGO   *(Going over to embrace* BUZZ *and* KAREN *warmly)* Oh? And who has the splendid job of standing by for the star who never misses a performance—knock on wood?

HOWARD   Eve.

MARGO   Eve? . . . *Eve?* *(She is taken aback and circles slowly behind* EVE*)* Well, I always knew you were interested in the theater, and in me, but I had no idea . . . Oh, yes, the Madison Dramatic Society . . . Pinter, Albee . . .

EVE   Miss Channing, I can't tell you how relieved I am that you arrived late . . . I would have dried up completely. I couldn't have gone on!

BUZZ   She gave a helluva reading.

KAREN   You would have been proud of her, too.

MARGO   *(Moving toward* BILL*)*   Oh? And were you proud of her, Bill?

BILL   Yes. I must say she really is an actress. It was a pleasant surprise.

MARGO   Surprise? *I'm* the only one in this group who's had a surprise. Little surprises being planned behind my back.

84

(She moves toward HOWARD*)*

HOWARD Cut that, Margo! No one's kept anything from you. We asked you to be here.

MARGO A pure formality. I'm sure it was all decided amongst you kiddies days and days ago . . . Or perhaps, Howard, during one of those magical evenings when you and Eve were dancing the night away!

HOWARD *(Furious)* That's enough! Send me your objections in writing! You haven't got understudy approval in your contract in the first place!

(He storms out the stage door)

MARGO *(Crossing again toward* BILL*)* I can't get over it. It's just beginning to sink in. This little prairie flower has been standing in the wings, studying my every move—every line for five months—and I never saw what she was really up to!

*(*BILL *exits to the dressing room)*

EVE *(Walking toward* MARGO, *who is leaning against the chaise)* Miss Channing, I know I could never be more than adequate in covering the part, but if you . . . *(On the verge of tears)* have any objections, naturally I wouldn't dream . . .

KAREN *(Holding* EVE*)* Wait . . . I'm taking you out for a drink. Come on, Buzz.

BUZZ In a minute. Let's get this settled. I was surprised, too. She was a revelation.

MARGO   Well, naturally, it must have been a revelation to have a somewhat younger character played by a somewhat younger actress.

BUZZ *(Guiltily)*   What are you talking about?

MARGO   It must have sounded so new and fresh to you. You probably could hardly recognize your own play.

BUZZ   The play is actor-proof!

MARGO   Actor-proof! If you knew the bits, the schtick, I have to dredge out of the vaudeville trunk to give the illusion that something amusing is going on . . .

(She sits on the chaise)

BUZZ   You empty-headed, conceited bass fiddle! You're just a body and a voice! Don't ever forget—I'm the brain!

(BUZZ starts to leave and is stopped by MARGO's words)

MARGO   Till the autopsy, there's no proof!

(He stamps out)

KAREN *(To MARGO)*   Margo, you've been kicking us all around long enough. Someone ought to give *you* a good swift one for a change!
(She leaves)

EVE *(Moving slowly toward* MARGO) Miss Channing . . .
if I ever dreamed that anything I did could possibly
cause you any unhappiness, or come between you and
your friends . . . please believe me.

MARGO *(In a low, weary voice)* Oh, I do. And I'm full of
admiration for you. *(Stands up and approaches* EVE) If
you can handle yourself on the stage with the same
artistry you display *off* the stage . . . well, my dear, you
are in the right place. *(She speaks the following lines as
the music of "Welcome to the Theater" begins)*

> Welcome to the theater,
> To the magic, to the fun!

> *(She sings)*

> Where painted trees and flowers grow,
> And laughter rings fortissimo,
> And treachery's sweetly done!

> Now you've entered the asylum,
> This profession unique,
> Actors are children
> Playing hide-and-ego-seek . . .

> So welcome, Miss Eve Harrington,
> To this business we call show,
> You're on your way
> To wealth and fame,
> Unsheath your claws,
> Enjoy the game!
> You'll be a bitch
> But they'll know your name
> From New York to Kokomo . . .

Welcome to the theater,
My dear, you'll love it so!

(EVE *exits, quietly defiant*)

Welcome to the dirty concrete hallways,
Welcome to the friendly roaches, too,
Welcome to the pinches from the stagehands,
It's the only quiet thing they do . . .
Welcome to the Philadelphia critics,
Welcome, Librium and Nembutal,
Welcome to a life of laryngitis,
Welcome to dark toilets in the hall . . .
Welcome to the flop
You thought would run for years,
Welcome to the world
Of tears and cheers and fears . . .

Welcome to the theater,
With some luck you'll be a pro,
You'll work and slave
And scratch and bite,
You'll learn to kill
With sheer delight,
You'll only come
Alive at night
When you're in a show!
Welcome to the theater,
You fool, you'll love it so.

(BILL *enters from the dressing room and goes to her*)

BILL (*In a kidding, comic tone, to cut through her mood*)
Hellooo, Margo.

MARGO (*Very down*)   Margo. What's that? Just a body and a voice.

BILL (*Puts his hands on her shoulders*)   What a body. What a voice.

MARGO   Imagine, she turns up out of nowhere, and gives a performance!

BILL   A reading.

MARGO (*Moving toward the chaise*)   A performance!

BILL (*Following* MARGO)   Margo, you've got to stop hurting yourself and me, the two of us. I—

MARGO (*Not listening, continuing her own line of thought, so that her speech and* BILL's *following speech are spoken at the same time*)   I'm in a dream scene in one of those movies! I'm screaming down an empty tunnel . . . no one can hear me . . . no one will listen to me . . .

BILL (*Continuing what he was saying*)   I love you! You're a beautiful intelligent actress at the peak of her career, and—

MARGO (*Interrupting*)   And all the time she's coming at me with a knife!

BILL   Margo!

MARGO   Why can't you see it?

BILL (*Takes her by the shoulders and sits her down at the end of the chaise*)   Margo! There are always young, talented people coming along, but you're *you*—you're unique! (*She struggles to get up, but he pushes her back on the chaise, pinning her down by the shoulders*) No one can possibly be a threat to you. It's beneath you to let an innocent girl like Eve turn you into a screaming harpy!

MARGO She turns me into a heavy! *(He walks away)* She's Snow White, and you're all those cute little dwarfs, and I wind up as the Wicked Witch! Why can't *I* be Snow White for a change!

BILL Ha! Anything! Bong! The fight's over. Calm down.

MARGO I will not calm down!

BILL Don't calm down.

MARGO You're being very tolerant, aren't you?

BILL Well, I'm trying.

MARGO *(Standing up and moving toward him)* I don't want to be tolerated, or plotted against! Get her out of my life! You think she's talented? Fine. Help her. Get her a job in a touring company—a film in Lebanon! Let her run around naked off-Broadway someplace. Anyplace . . . Just away from *me* and away from *you!*

BILL *(Going toward the chaise)* Are you still on that! You can't really believe—

MARGO *(She follows, and they're now at opposite ends of the chaise)* What else am I going to believe! The girl turns up out of nowhere, inexperienced, amateur at best, and gives a performance that knocks everybody out— rehearsed, I have no doubt, over and over, day and night . . . full of those personal, unmistakable Bill Sampson touches!

(MARGO *moves away*)

BILL (*Exploding, following* MARGO)   Goddamn it! I've had it up to here! I'm sick to death of your paranoiac outbursts!

MARGO   Paranoiac—what a hangup on a word! I don't even know what it means!

BILL   Well, it's time you found out! Go to an analyst!

MARGO   Go to hell!

(*There is tense silence*)

BILL (*Quietly*)   We usually wind up screaming and throwing things as the curtain comes down, then it comes up again and everything's fine. But not this time. Good-bye, Margo.

(*He goes to the stage door*)

MARGO   Where are you going, Bill? Mustn't keep the kid waiting.

BILL   Paranoia.

(*He slams the door.* MARGO *stands alone on the empty stage*)

MARGO (*Singing*)
Where painted trees and flowers grow . . .
And laughter rings fortissimo,
And treachery's sweetly done.
Welcome to the theater,
You fool, you love it so.

Curtain

Act Two

The scene is BUZZ *and* KAREN'*s Connecticut home, a few weeks later. The curtain goes up on the living room. The right wall is dominated by a large stone fireplace. Downstage of the fireplace is a cushioned chair with a small banjo on the wall behind the chair . . .*

In the middle of the set is a comfortable-looking built-in sofa. There is a railing above which guards the landing leading to the kitchen, off to the right. In front of the sofa is a large coffee table. To the left of the sofa is a section between the sofa and the steps to the landing. It has two levels, one with a yellow cushion for sitting and the other, higher, holding a large lamp, a phone, a Brandy decanter, three coffee mugs, and two plastic glasses.

Three steps on the left of the set lead to a landing. To the right of the landing is another step that goes to the kitchen landing. This landing is against the back wall, in the center of which is a window with floor-length drapes. The door to the outside is left of the window.

KAREN *is alone, looking out the window at the snow. She is highly excited, drinking, and slightly tipsy. The phone rings, and she rushes to answer it.*

KAREN   Hello? . . . Eve! Glad you called back. You're at the theater already? . . . Good . . . No, nothing went wrong—you'll definitely go on tonight! I *told* you I'd find a way! (*Sits*) Here's what I did. Buzz is driving Margo to the station, but they'll never get there. No gas in the car . . . I emptied it! It can't go more than a mile . . .

Eve, there's no need to feel guilty. You simply said the
most direct way to show Margo is to have the curtain go
up and the play to go on just once without her. (*Gets up*)
Well, tonight's the night! So keep calm, act surprised.
I'm just sick I have to miss it . . . Don't thank me, Eve.
We *both* thought of it. We're in it together! 'Bye. Good
luck! (KAREN *hangs up and takes a sip of her drink. She
puts three cups out on the coffee table, realizes her error,
and quickly takes one away. She sings "Inner Thoughts"*)

> Just a prank, some harmless fun,
> We'll laugh about it when it's done,
> Won't we, Margo?
> Sure we will!
> Funny, I feel guilty now,
> As if I'd been had somehow,
> Could it have a thing to do with Eve?
> No, that's silly,
> Really silly,
> Eve's too sweet and too naïve.

> > (KAREN *goes up the steps toward the kitchen area.
> > The door opens, and in walks* BUZZ, *followed by*
> > MARGO, *both bundled up and freezing*)

Buzz? . . . Margo!

MARGO (*At the top of the steps*)   Any mail for me while
I was gone?

KAREN   What happened?

BUZZ (*Crossing to the fireplace*)   Car ran out of gas. I was
an idiot not to check it.

KAREN   It never happened before. But the train . . . did you miss it?

MARGO (*Walking down the steps*)   No, I'm on it. This is just a photograph of me. I can't believe it. (*Approaching the fireplace*) I can't believe this has happened to me. Karen, what a thing to do!

KAREN (*Alarmed*)   Wh—what do you mean?

MARGO   I know you come to the country for peace and quiet, but this is ridiculous! There isn't another human being for a thousand miles around.

(*She warms herself by the fire*)

BUZZ (*Crossing to the phone*)   I'll call the theater . . . tell them what happened. What time is it?

KAREN   Twenty to eight. I'll get you some hot coffee.

(*She exits to the kitchen*)

BUZZ (*Sings "Inner Thoughts" to himself, moving downstage*)

It's a rotten thing to say,
But I'd love to see my play
Without Margo,
Just one time!

(MARGO *takes off her coat and puts it on the sofa*)

I'm an egocentric jerk,

But I wonder—would it work?
Would my words sound fresh and great and new?
Buzz, you're evil,
Evil, *evil!*
After all that Margo's done for you!

(KAREN *re-enters*)

MARGO You mean we're stuck here?

KAREN (*At the top of the steps*) Yes.

MARGO You'd better stand back. At eight-thirty I start doing the play no matter where I am!

BUZZ (*Crosses back to the phone and dials*) I'm sorry, Margo. I'm sorry for me. I'm such a stingy bastard, I'm thinking of all those refunds at the box office.

(KAREN *walks over to* MARGO *and hands her a cup*)

KAREN Here's your coffee.

(MARGO *sits on the chair, and* KAREN *kneels next to the coffee table*)

MARGO Coffee! Hey, there's a coffee commercial I'm supposed to do tomorrow, and I've been counting on the loot. Damnit!

BUZZ (*On the phone*) Hello, backstage? . . . Hello, Bert. Hold on. I've got some incredible news. Margo's stuck here with us in Connecticut. Car broke down. Blame me, I'm guilty! . . . Oh, good . . . (*To* MARGO *and* KAREN) Eve got there early tonight.

MARGO (*Crossing to the phone*) Let me talk to her.

(KAREN *reacts*)

BUZZ Bert, can she come to the phone? . . . Oh, good . . .
(*Handing the phone to* MARGO) She's right there.

MARGO (*Sits on the landing steps*) Hello, Eve? . . . Of
course you're nervous. Who wouldn't be. But listen, if
you can remember all of Dana Andrews' lines from my
old movies, you can certainly remember these. Now look,
that quick change in Act Three, it's a killer. Be sure to
kick your shoes off *before* you step into the dress or you'll
get all fouled up. Duane will help you. Okay? . . . good
luck.

(*She hangs up*)

BUZZ Margo, that was nice.

MARGO Was it? I thought it was minimally civilized.
What's nice is your asking the body and the voice up for
the weekend after all the rotten things she said about
the brain.

(BUZZ *goes over to* KAREN)

BUZZ We can't stay angry at each other. Sometimes I
want to murder you, but only temporarily. We know
you too well.

(BUZZ *kisses* KAREN *on the forehead*)

MARGO (*Sings "Inner Thoughts" to herself*)

99

So you know me, good for you,
How I wish that I did too,
Margo Channing,
Who is she?

    (BUZZ *goes to the sofa*)

Now the play's about to start,
Eve is going to play my part!
Bill is there—I wonder what he thinks?
Wouldn't it be
Just terrific
If he thought she really stinks?

    (KAREN *picks up* MARGO's *cup to hand it to her*)

KAREN   Drink your coffee, Margo. (MARGO *is silent*) It's only one performance.

MARGO   It isn't that.

KAREN   Bill? You two have had fights before.

MARGO   This one was special. I guess I got suspicious and jealous of Eve because of her age. And *his* age . . . And *my* age.

KAREN   Come on, Bill's not that much younger than you.

MARGO   He's thirty-three. He looked the same three years ago and he'll look the same thirty years from now. I hate men.

KAREN (*Now at the sofa*)   I'm sure he'll be back as usual.

BUZZ Of course he will. *(To lighten the mood, he goes and pours a drink)* All right, we're here for the night, so let's enjoy it. All those who want to watch "Beat the Clock" raise hands! Monopoly? You wanna smoke some grass?

KAREN Have you got some?

BUZZ *(Moving toward the chair near the fireplace)* No, just seeing if you were paying attention.

MARGO *(Going up to the top of the steps, laughing)* Well, if I finally had to miss a performance, it couldn't have happened in a nicer way . . . with a couple of people I love.

BUZZ That really calls for a toast. *(Raising his brandy glass)* To friendship! *(He drains the glass and dashes it into the fireplace. It bounces back unbroken. They all stare at it)* I mean, to plastic. I mean, to the real things in life.
  (BUZZ takes his banjo off the wall. He sits on the arm of the chair. The three of them sing "Good Friends")

BUZZ
      When you've got good friends,
      You've got a good life,
      Think about that.
      When you've got good friends . . .

KAREN Buzz, you're getting sentimental . . .

BUZZ
> You've got it all!

MARGO   Hold on, you're getting to me.

BUZZ
> For when life is cruel,
> And they call you fool,
> You're not alone,
> If you've got good friends
> On whom you can call!
>
> Good friends, who couldn't care less,
> If you're a failure, or a success,
> They're there,
> Whatever you do,
> They like you for you!
> Not your money or your gorgeousness!
>
> Friendship is a ring,
> A circular thing,
> It never ends,
> So kick off your shoes,
> You're with good friends!
> You're with good friends!

MARGO	BUZZ and KAREN
Life is full of frets,	Good friends,
Remorse and regrets,	Good friends,
Doors that are locked.	You're poor without
When you've got good friends,	Good friends,
You've got the key!	People you love,
	People you trust,
	You've got the key!

BUZZ   KAREN and MARGO

As you go through life   Do-do, do-do,
There's three things you need,   Do-do, do-do,
Money is one,   Do-do, do-do do.
Number two is sex,   All the way.
You know number three!

BUZZ, KAREN and MARGO

Good friends,
Who really don't care,
If you're a swinger,
Or you're a square!

MARGO

I know that you two,
You never could do
One mean thing to me!

KAREN (*Moves away from* BUZZ *and* MARGO; *to herself*)
Oh, I wish I'd never drained that tank . . .

BUZZ, KAREN, and MARGO

Friendship is a ring,
A circular thing,
It never ends,
And we've got it good,
We've got good friends!

MARGO

Without you life is empty!

KAREN (*Guiltily, to herself*) Empty!

BUZZ
>
Hey, baby, you're a gas!

MARGO   T'anks!

KAREN *(With growing remorse)*   Gas tanks!

MARGO
>
It's just like New Year's Eve!

KAREN   Eve? Eve! Gas! Empty! Tanks! What have I done
to my . . . ahh . . .

MARGO and BUZZ
>
Good friends!

> (KAREN *sinks to the floor in a faint*)

MARGO and BUZZ *(Surprised)*   Good God!

Blackout

SCENE TWO

EVE, BERT, *and* STAN HARDING *enter as the dressing-room set comes on behind them.* EVE *is wearing the pailletted evening dress that* MARGO *wore in Scene Five, and it seems made for her. She is heady with excitement, and though still under control, she is ready to get carried away with her instant success.*

BERT   The rest of the cast was twice as nervous as you were. You didn't even make a wrong move! It was like you'd been playing it forever.

EVE   Did you hear them! Did you hear that audience!

STAN   Terrific, Eve. Star-dust time, believe me.

EVE   Oh, thank you, Mr. Harding . . .

STAN   I want to do a story on you for the column. Meet me at Joe Allen's later, will you?

   (*He starts to leave*)

EVE   I'll be there!

STAN (*At the door*)   And don't forget it, I discovered you first.

   (*He exits.* DUANE *enters from the bathroom*)

BERT   What else can I say? You're a young Margo.

EVE *(Coldly)*   Really?

DUANE   Well, I have to admit it . . . You wowed them.

EVE *(Surprised, moving to the dressing table)*   Thank you,
Duane. Funny . . . tonight I was going to take a chance
and just phone in. Good thing I changed my mind and
turned up early.

DUANE *(Picks up his coat from the chair)*   Yeah. But how
come the columnists and critics turned up? A little birdie
must have told them . . . maybe a vulture.

   (He exits)

BERT *(Adoringly)*   It was one of those nights. I guess I had
a little something to do with it . . .

   (He moves toward her to embrace her)

EVE *(Sliding out of it coolly)*   Oh, did you?

   (There is a knock, and BILL looks in)

BILL   Hello . . .

   (EVE looks thrilled at seeing BILL)

BERT   Terrific, wasn't she, Mr. Sampson?

BILL   Yeah!

BERT   Uh . . . I'll wait for you Eve.

EVE *(Sweetly evasive)* Well, I don't think so . . . I feel so . . . well, you know . . .

BERT *(Grimly)* Ohhh . . .G'night.
(*Exits looking at* BILL'*s back, disgruntled.* EVE *turns to* BILL)

BILL Well, what I said after Act Two still goes. None of the earmarks of a one-shot performance. It's there.

EVE *(Looking radiantly into his eyes)* Oh, Mr. Sampson . . .

BILL You know, I've been spending all my time splicing strips of film together in a dark little room. Almost forgot what live theater can be—the excitement when someone up there makes contact with the audience! Have a good time tonight. You deserve it. *(Kisses her forehead)* Good night, Eve. *(He starts to go out)*

EVE Bill . . .

BILL *(Stopping)* Yes?

EVE *(Walking toward him)*
Thank you. *(Sings)*
 The best night of my life
 Is here, is now . .
 (Speaking)
I couldn't have done it without you.

BILL *(Surprised)* Without *me?* Come *on* . . . I stopped by and gave you a five-minute pep talk before the curtain went up . . .

EVE *(Sitting on the sofa)* Something you said made the whole difference. Without it, I might have been just plain embarrassing.

BILL *(Sitting on the arm of the sofa)* Really? what was that?

EVE You said, "The one thing that makes an audience uncomfortable is to see an actor pressing—sweating to make good." You said, "If you feel you're losing them, don't panic. Hold very still inside. Don't go after them; make them come to you."

BILL *(Smiling)* And that's what did it?

EVE I held on to that as if I were holding on to you. It meant everything to me—and so do you.

(She does just that, putting her hand on top of his)

BILL *(Gets up and moves away)* Well, that's a very comprehensive statement.

EVE *(Gets up and slowly follows BILL. They face each other, very close)* Do you remember the night Greta Garbo met Sigmund Freud? I think it's time Bill Sampson met Eve Harrington.

(There is a slight pause)

BILL You're quite a girl.

EVE You think . . . ?

BILL But I've *got* a girl. Remember Margo?

EVE *(Confidently)*   I'll never forget her. That's how I met *you*. Anyway, you're not together at the moment . . . Maybe this is *my* moment.

BILL   Do you mean *our* moment?

EVE *(Starts to put her arms up around his neck)*   Let's find out.

BILL *(Evenly)*   Only thing is . . . you're pressing . . . I think you've lost me. *(He steps back, out of her embrace)* Remember, Eve, offstage as well as on: don't go after them; make them come to you.

> *(He leaves.* EVE, *shocked and humiliated, recoils for a moment. Then, in a tearful rage, she hurls her shoes at the door, pulls the curtain across the room, and half pulls her dress off.* HOWARD *knocks on the door)*

EVE *(Shouting in anger)*   Who is it?

HOWARD *(Entering)*   A flabbergasted and very lucky producer.

EVE *(Pulling herself together, instantly)*   Come in, Mr. Benedict.

HOWARD *(Goes to closet and gets his coat)*   I thought this only happened in those old Ruby Keeler movies. But tonight the understudy took over and turned a potential lynch mob into a cheering squad.

EVE (*Getting her arms out of her dress and holding it up against her*) I'm so glad you came back. In all the confusion, I forgot to thank you for the flowers.

HOWARD My pleasure. I just came back for my coat.

(EVE *pulls open the curtain*)

EVE Are you still free? I've had a change of plans.

HOWARD (*Looking her over*) Great, then we shall celebrate. My apartment. I've a bottle of Mumm's Cordon Rouge cooling on ice.

EVE No, let's go to Joe Allen's. I feel like being with the gypsies.

HOWARD (*Puts his coat on a chair*) Eve, you're a very clever girl. I came through for you, giving you the understudy part . . .

EVE (*Quickly*) Haven't I come through for you by giving a good performance? We are friends, aren't we?

HOWARD Yes, heavens knows, we're friends.

EVE I have no illusions about tonight. It was just one performance. It could be forgotten tomorrow.

HOWARD (*Moves in behind her*) Not necessarily. After Margo leaves, I could give you a crack at taking over the part.

EVE (*Bursting out*) I don't want her hand-me-downs!

HOWARD (*Preparing to leave, he picks up his coat*) Hm.
You've gone up considerably in your esteem in the last
—uh—three seconds.

EVE (*Recovering herself*) I'm sorry to sound so unappreci-
ative, but if I'm to go on with this, I want a part of my
own—or nothing.

HOWARD (*Turning and facing her*) Perhaps even something like that can be arranged. (EVE, *holding her dress
up against her, crosses and takes her street dress from the
closet, puts it down on the chair, and facing him, begins
to unzip and take off the evening dress. Sings*)

So thank you
For the best night of my life.

(*Slowly the dress slips to the floor*)

The scene is Joe Allen's. The GYPSIES *have moved their chairs and tables into position.* STAN *enters.* DANNY, BONNIE, *and* DUANE *are down front on the right. They talk as the set comes on and the tables are arranged.*

BONNIE Well, did the audience just get up and leave when they announced Margo Channing wasn't going to appear?

DUANE They groaned a lot, but most of them stayed.

DANNY Really?

DUANE Well, what are they gonna do? They wrote in September for their seats, finally got a pair in February. They've already paid the baby-sitter, made the trek in by dog sled, wolfed down a six-course dinner in twenty minutes. They can't leave—they're exhausted! Anyway, what's their choice? Go out on Eighth Avenue and get mugged? They'd stay to see *me* in the part. (*Starts to go and stops*) And I wouldn't be bad.

GYPSY GIRL (*At another table*) But, Duane, how was she?

DUANE (*Begrudgingly*) A sensation!

> (EVE *and* HOWARD *enter, and the* GYPSIES *applaud.* STAN *greets and leads them to a table. All three sit,* EVE *in the center*)

STAN   Well, how do you feel?

EVE *(Buoyantly)*   Fantastic!

DANNY *(Coming to their table)*   Excuse me, Mr. Benedict.
Eve, we're all so excited for you. Can you come over . . .
We'd like to buy you a drink!

EVE *(Sweetly, but distantly)*   Not now, Danny. I'm busy.
Maybe later.

(DANNY *retreats*)

DANNY *(To the others at his table)*   I just got the hello-but-
don't-come-over bit.

STAN   They're all gonna want to meet you. Tonight, for my
money, you had ten times as much heart as Miss Channing. And there wasn't a man who didn't have the hots
for ya . . . That's a compliment. I'll put it more delicately
in the column.

HOWARD   We rely on your good taste, Stan. *(A waiter
dashes by)* Uh, waiter! Excuse me . . . I'll deal directly
with the bar.

(He goes to the bar)

STAN *(Taking notes)*   To continue, Miss Harrington,
you're the right age for the part.

EVE   Mr. Harding, I do want to make one thing clear. I
adore Margo Channing, and I only hope I'll have the
energy and grace she has, when *I'm* her age. I mean, she

represents an old theatrical tradition, when a star was a
star! I do think today, however, in contemporary plays,
that must be dropped, and young actresses given a
chance to . . .

(*Two* GYPSIES *come over*)

FIRST GYPSY   Excuse us, Eve, we're dying to know what
it . .

SECOND GYPSY *(His words overlapping)*   How'd it feel?
Were you nervous?

EVE   Hi, kids. I won't be very long. *(The boys withdraw)*
Of course, mature actresses are sometimes also childlike,
self-deluded people. They don't realize that they can be
personally brilliant yet detrimental to the play, and—

BONNIE *(Rushing over)*   Eve! We heard you were sen-
sational . . . !

EVE *(Icily)*   Please! Not now! Can't you see I'm busy . . .
trying to answer a few questions!

(BONNIE *bumps into* HOWARD, *returning with the
drinks*)

BONNIE   Excuse me! Oh, Mr. Benedict, I just wanted to—

EVE *(Getting up)*   Howard, you were right. We really
should go someplace quieter. Do you mind, Mr. Harding?

STAN *(Rising)*   Not at all. Howard?

(They start toward the door. EVE *and* BONNIE *come face to face.* EVE *haughtily walks around her and out, the* GYPSIES *watching)*

BONNIE *(Mimicking the grand manner* EVE *took on as she walks over to one of the tables)* Kids . . . she was *merely* trying to answer a few questions! *(The* GYPSIES *hoot)* Pull-ease, kids, not now. I'm *busy!*
    (She sits. The music begins playing. DUANE *grabs a pad and pencil and sits across from* BONNIE*)*

DUANE   Hello, Miss Starshine. I'm from *Screw Magazine,* and our readers would like to know if success will change you.

BONNIE   No, I plan to be as obnoxious as I ever was!

DUANE   And you'll remember your old friends?

BONNIE   Of course. I'll never forget them. And I'll never see them either!

DUANE *(Begins singing "She's No Longer a Gypsy)*

She's no longer a gypsy,
She'll be leaving us soon,
She did the understudy-to-the-rescue bit,
Now she's halfway to the moon!

She's no longer a gypsy,
No more Equity calls,
She's gonna get them crazy invitations now
To Truman Capote's balls . . .

GYPSIES
> Have a beer,
> Your last one, dear,
> From this night on it's all champagne!

BONNIE
> The star was late,
> And I was great!

ALL
> You got up early

DUANE
> And pulled a Shirley MacLaine!

BONNIE
> I'm no longer a gypsy,
> Put me on the marquee!
> It's out-of-the-chorus-into-heaven time . . .

GYPSIES
> It should happen,
> It should only happen,
> God, let it happen to me!

ALL *(To the sound of samba music)*
> Aye yi yi yi,
> Aye yi, aye yi . . .
> She's no longer a gypsy!
> It's the magic of Broadway,
> Overnight you're a star.

DUANE
> Now ev'ry jerk who ever turned you down will claim
> He made you what you are!

GIRLS

No more automat coffee,

BONNIE

It's the Plaza for tea.

GYPSIES

You did the "Hey-world-now-you're-gonna see-me" bit!

DUANE

"I tell you, Manny, with this kid we got a hit!"

ALL

It's that good old overnight sensation shit!
It should happen,
It should only happen,
God, let it happen to me.

She's no longer a gypsy,
She'll be leaving the street.
Hey, she's a regular Mitzi Gaynor now,
Don't you love them dancing feet!

(A *wildly competitive dance number follows*)

Fame,
Success,
Autographs,
Me . . . please God!

Who?
Broadway . . . Hollywood!
Money, money!
Thank you, thank you!
Me!
Me!
Me!

What is it that we're living for?
Applause! Applause!
Nothing I know
Brings on the glow
Like sweet applause.

DUANE (*In a hammy baritone*)
One alone to be my own.

> (BONNIE *hits* DUANE *over the head with a sledge-hammer. As the number progresses, the other dancers follow suit; every time one of them gets into the spotlight, he is quickly done away with.* BONNIE *has now acquired a blond wig, dark glasses, a fur stole, and a cigarette holder, and she sits in a glamorous pose away from the crowd*)

ALL (*Bowing modestly*)   Thank you. Thank you. Thank you. Thank you. Thank you. Thank you.
Star me—
To hell with you!

Kill—
For big chance!

Hut, two, three, four!
Enemy in sight!
Ready, aim, fire!

GYPSIES
She's no longer a gypsy,
It's good-bye to the bunch!

BONNIE
And if you ever get to Beverly Hills,
Don't drop in for lunch!

ALL

> Treat her nice,
> La, la, la!
> That's our advice,
> La, la, la!
> You take care of this dear girl!

DUANE

> I'm telling you,
> She will come through,
> But if she doesn't,
> Why not give *me* a whirl?

ALL

> She's no longer a gypsy,
> Put her on the marquee!

BONNIE

> I'll get to meet George Jessel
> At a Friar's roast!

DUANE

> You'll be a big fat star
> And have the world on toast,

ALL

> But don't forget your friends
> Who love you most!

> *(At this point all the dancers kill each other off with machine guns, daggers, dart guns, etc., and finally the stage is piled high with bodies, with* BONNIE *posing on top, triumphant)*

> It should happen,

It should only happen,
God, let it happen to me!

*(The number ends; then the music resumes as the
dancers exit, chanting)*

It should happen to me,
It should happen to me,
It should happen to me,
It should happen to me.

DUANE

Ev'ry body's part gypsy,
Ev'ry body I know,
Oh, even I have dreamed
That I could leap onstage,
And really stop the show!

*(As the scene changes, a motion-picture cameraman
enters stage center and BONNIE and DUANE vie for
the most advantageous position in front of the lens,
pushing each other aside. Finally DUANE carries
her off, protesting all the way. As they exit, the
living-room set comes into position)*

MARGO's *living room. It is mid-afternoon the following day; the place is set up for an El Dorado Coffee commercial. Present are the* TV DIRECTOR, *the cameraman, a script girl, and an assistant.*

MARGO, *wearing a simple yellow dress, looks tense and tired. She is seated on the sofa, holding a cup and saucer. On the coffee table are a jar of El Dorado Instant Coffee, a tin of El Dorado Regular, and a coffee server. TV lights are at each end of the sofa; the movie camera is directed at* MARGO.

Watching from the terrace are KAREN *and* PETER. KAREN's *coat is draped over the brick wall. There are coffee cups in front of them, and* KAREN *is holding a folded newspaper. She shows her uneasiness throughout the scene. The script girl walks to the edge of the terrace and sits.*

DIRECTOR *(To the right of the camera)*   A little higher with the cup. Now raise it and take a sip. Now let's have that famous look over the rim of the cup . . . Good . . . Now put it down That was perfect, Miss Channing, thank you. *(Walking over to the script girl by the terrace)* Just so you'll know, over that shot we hear the voice saying, "As an actress and star, Margo Channing is one-of-a-kind. So when she entertains at home, she always serves the one-of-a-kind coffee, El Dorado."

MARGO *(Depressed)* All right. *(Gets up from the sofa)* Is that it?

DIRECTOR *(Crosses to the sofa)* No, that was for El Dorado Regular Grind. We still have to do El Dorado Freeze-Dried and El Dorado Drip.

MARGO I'm sorry, it's just that running in from the country, getting dressed in thirty seconds . . . I'm . . .

DIRECTOR That's all right, Miss Channing, you're doing fine. Take a few minutes.

> *(The script girl rises, removes the cup and saucer from the coffee table, and goes off to the kitchen, returning with two cups and saucers which she places on the coffee table. Then she takes away the coffee and returns, walking behind the camera.* MARGO *joins* PETER *and* KAREN*)*

MARGO Couldn't we finish this tomorrow?

PETER You know that's out of the question. They're here; get it over with. I don't want you to blow this. It's—

MARGO *(Moving between* KAREN *and* PETER*)* Yes, I know —it's dignified, it's got residuals, it's security for my old age, which judging from this morning's paper I'm in the middle of right now.

PETER Aw, Margo . . .

KAREN   I can't believe Eve would say those things.

MARGO (*Reading from a newspaper taken from* KAREN)
"Miss Harrington, while restating her admiration for Miss
Channing, lamented the fact that mature actresses can
be so self-deluded, they keep playing younger parts with
detrimental results to the play." Detrimental, self-deluded.
Does that sound like Stan Harding?

PETER   So someone bumraps you in a column. It stinks
but . . .

MARGO   What gets me is how the papers and TV people
happened to catch that particular performance.

PETER   Well, first performance you ever missed. That's
instant news.

MARGO   So she got good notices. I hate it, but I can face
it. But what about this from Stan . . . (*Reading*) "Miss
Harrington was a radiant, natural young angel up there
tonight. Quite a difference from Miss Channing, cleverly
bundled up in her high-necked gowns, designed to con-
ceal; and discreetly lit with all the pink gelatins in town,
to create the illusion of youth." My God, she wore my
costumes, and the lighting was exactly the same. It's so
rotten—so unfair.
     (*She gives the paper to* PETER)

DIRECTOR   Can we go, Miss Channing?

MARGO (*With a little laugh*)   I guess I'd better, or it'll be
all over town that I'm too feeble to work. (BILL *walks in
and is standing at the side.* MARGO *doesn't see him and*

goes to sit on the couch again) Okay, fellas! Let's get in there for that one-of-a-kind coffee! Get this one-of-a-kind profile before it crumbles. *(She lifts the cup, but she is trembling, and the cup falls and breaks)* I'm sorry.

(She gets up. The script-girl picks up the pieces of broken cup and exits to the kitchen)

BILL *(Going to her quickly)* Margo.

MARGO Bill . . .

(She goes to him and he takes her in his arms. KAREN takes her coat from the wall and puts it on)

BILL I read that piece of garbage. It's not even worth a tear. And you were right about that girl.

MARGO Bill, I'm so tired.

DIRECTOR Look, these things happen. We'll just leave everything here and pick up those two shots tomorrow.

PETER Yes, do it tomorrow. That's *my* suggestion.

(The TV people and PETER exit. KAREN, nervously working her way toward the door, bumps into the swivel chair)

KAREN *(Trying to hide her feelings of guilt)* Bill, I'm so glad you're here. She's had a terrible morning. *(MARGO sits on the sofa)* I had no idea . . . Well, now that you're here, I'll . . . Margo, call me later if there's anything . . . well, call me. So long.

BILL   So long, Karen. (*She exits.* BILL *tries to pull* MARGO *out of her depression*) I only dropped by because I wanted a cup of coffee. (*Takes his coat off and puts it on the small chair*) Come now, I want that coffee, and I want it poured by you, right now. (*Picks up the clapboard*) All right, we're rolling! Take one—Margo sad! (*Looks through the camera*) Cut! Perfect! Take two—Margo— glad! (*Looks through the camera again.* MARGO *has the same sad expression*) Cut! (*Like a wild foreign director*) Nothing! You're not doing it right. I want beeg smile! Plenty teeth! (*She grins*) More, more! (*She grins more and more*) No, not insanity! Cut! I got an easy one for you. Margo sexy! (MARGO *is lying down. He pans in on her*) Margo no feel sexy? Margo sad? (*She nods*) Sad Margo. (*She holds up her hands, witchlike, as if to scratch*) Evil Margo! Margo, the Wicked Witch! (*She does a funny witch's cackle, joining in his game, and snaps out of her depression*) Bravo! You're everything the slogan promises!

(*He takes her hand and pulls her up on the back of the couch. He jumps over to sit beside her, and sings a gay, lilting waltz, "One of a Kind"*)

You're one of a kind,
A fabulous bird,
You're out of your mind
And 'way out of sight.
You're one of a kind,
Unique is the word,
And that's why I find
The others all trite . . .

(*Puts his arm around her*)

I like the weird things that happen

Inside of your skull,
Being with you may be hard on the nerves,

(Her head is on his shoulder)

But it's never dull,
No, sir, never dull . . .

(He stands up on the sofa)

You walk in a room,
The people all stare,

(She stands up on the sofa)

'Cause, baby, you bloom.
They'd have to be blind

(He jumps down)

To not recognize
The rarest of rare
Right under their eyes,
You're one of a kind!

(Goes to the light on the right, turns it on, and indicates a model's pose. She rejects the idea)

If there were two of you,
Or, God forbid, a few of you,

(Circles the camera and looks through it)

Too much is what it would be,
But you're one of a kind,

(MARGO gets off the sofa, and BILL goes to join her)

One of a kind,
One of a kind,

One of a kind,
And you're the kind of a woman for me!

Who else would take a swim completely dressed
In Central Park at three A.M.
The night she won the Tony?

MARGO (*Turning*)   I didn't do that . . .

BILL
Well, you did!

MARGO
Who grabbed a flaming cherries jubilee
And burned a movie script at Chasen's,
Yelling it was phony!

BILL   Was that me?

MARGO   Um hmmmm . . .

BILL and MARGO (*Singing side by side*)
You always were a crazy kid!

(*Now with their backs together*)

I shudder at the things you did!

BILL
Your ego seems to suit my id . . .

MARGO
So kiss me!

BILL   You mad fool! (*Picking up* MARGO)
You know you grind your teeth at night.

MARGO
Your snoring is a real delight.

BILL and MARGO

It's noisy, but we sleep all right!

(*Bill puts her down and fakes a hurt back*)

You . . .
Are . . .
One of a kind,
A fabulous bird,
You're out of your mind,
And 'way out of sight!
You're one of a kind,
Unique is the word,
And that's why I find
The others all trite . . .

MARGO (*Waltzes across the stage*)
At times you're selfish and stubborn
And blind as a mole,

(*Turns*)

But even so, you're a kick to be with,
You're good for my soul,
So good for my soul . . .

BILL and MARGO (*Doing a two-step*)
You walk in a room,
The people all stare,

'Cause, baby, you bloom.
They'd have to be blind
To not recognize
The rarest of rare
Right under their eyes,
You're one of a kind!

MARGO
If there were two of you,
Or, God forbid, a few of you,
Too much is what it would be!

BILL and MARGO
But you're one of a kind,
One of a kind,
One of a kind,
One of a kind,

    (They strike a dance pose)

And you're the kind of a nut

    (They kiss)

For me!

    (They do an eccentric little waltz clog and finish it
    by striking a Ballet Russe pose. They kiss happily
    for a long time)

MARGO *(As if in a dream)* Bill?

BILL Mmmmmmmmmm . . . ?

    (He is kissing her face and neck)

MARGO   Bill . . . tell me one thing?

BILL (*Still kissing her*)   Yes?

MARGO   Was she good?

BILL   Who?

MARGO   You were there last night. Eve . . . was she that good?

BILL   Forget it.

(*He kisses her*)

MARGO (*Through the kiss*)   Well, *was* she?

BILL (*Breaking from her and moving a couple of steps away*) Yes, she was good. So *that's* what you're thinking about.

MARGO   I can't very well help it, can I?

BILL   I'm kissing you, thinking of nothing but you, and *that's* what's racing around in your mind!

MARGO   You and me—that's on my mind, too.

(*They go toward the sofa. She sits*)

BILL   Yeah! In the bottom drawer someplace. You certainly know how to make a fella feel wanted and loved. What the hell's the matter with me! Why do I keep coming back and getting kicked in the teeth? Because I keep thinking each time things are going to be different! That you're going to change!

MARGO   But I don't want you to change, Bill. I want you just as you are. I've missed you so. (*She pulls him down next to her*) Who else is going to catch me every time I fall off the high wire? (*She puts his arm around her and her head on his shoulder*) Do me a favor, Bill . . . marry me?

BILL (*After a pause*)   No. You don't need me, my love . . . you need a safety net. The answer is no.

MARGO (*Sitting up*)   I knew you'd get cold feet if I ever really—

BILL   It's just that for the first time I'm facing it honestly. Why should you change? How can you? A lifetime of conditioning since you were nineteen, defending your own little place up on top. It's a full-time job. (*Gets up and moves away*) Marrying you would be bigamy. You're already married. You're a star . . . *that* comes first.

MARGO (*Gets up*)   Well, what do you want? A little wifey-poo waiting for you in the kitchen, knee-deep in lasagna?

BILL   Yeah, I guess I do. (*Suddenly very unhappy*) No, I don't. Because then it wouldn't be you, and you're the one I love. I'd be miserable. Damn it! There isn't any solution . . . (*Walks toward her*) Go take a nap, you must be exhausted. You do have to face your public in a couple of hours.

MARGO   You're right. And I'd better look particularly dazzling tonight. Will you pick me up afterward? (*There is a brief silence*)

BILL   I'm working late.

MARGO   When will I see you?

BILL   I don't know.

MARGO *(Pleading)*   Bill, I love you.

> *(She starts going toward her bedroom)*

BILL   I wish you could realize what a rival a fellow has in you.

MARGO *(Partway up the steps)*   I just don't understand.

> *(She exits. BILL looks after her, thoughtfully)*

BILL *(Singing)*
We were doing fine,
I thought we'd be okay.
Once it was you and me . . .
Now where the hell are we?
Two people who can't be . . .
Together.

> *Blackout*

SCENE FIVE

The scene takes place backstage, two weeks later. As the lights come up, EVE *enters between the proscenium and the backstage wall. She is wearing an attractive red dress, and radiates total confidence. She walks toward the center of the stage, and looks around possessively.* BERT, *who is standing next to the spiral staircase, sees her and approaches her from behind.*

BERT   Eve?

EVE *(Startled by his voice, turns to face him)*   Oh, hello, Bert! I just came by to pick up my things.

BERT   At midnight?

EVE   I wanted to be sure everyone had gone. My make-up box is in Margo's room someplace. I left it there the night I went on.

BERT   The two weeks since then have been pretty tense.

EVE *(Goes toward the chaise)*   Well, you should be glad I'm leaving.

BERT *(Grimly)*   You were pretty nice to me for a while. As long as it took to get rid of the understudy. I've served my purpose.

EVE (*Turning to face him*)   I've got to get my things.

BERT   Then you struck out with Bill Sampson . . . moved in fast on Buzz Richards.

EVE   That's foolish, dangerous gossip. You could hurt a lot of people with lies like that. (*Puts her coat down on the chaise*) Good-bye, Bert.

BERT   Good luck.

EVE   Don't worry. I'll be back in this theater, or another— and with my own understudy.

(*She exits to the dressing room*)

BERT   You're quite a girl. (BUZZ *enters through the stage door and heads for the dressing room, not seeing* BERT) Hello, Mr. Richards!

BUZZ (*Spinning around, guiltily*)   Hello, Bert.

BERT   Looking for someone?

BUZZ   No . . . I . . . I was just . . . How's the show going?

BERT   We should sell tickets to what goes on *after* the show.

(*He exits through the stage door.* EVE *comes out of the dressing room with her bag*)

BUZZ   Eve! (*She runs into his arms and they kiss eagerly*) I got delayed finishing those rewrites in Act One—the ones we talked about last night. God! I couldn't sleep, thinking about the way you read Leslie. The more I work on it, the more I know the girl is you.

EVE   I know! I feel it, too!

BUZZ   The play's ready to go; Howard doesn't want Margo to leave this one. What can stand in the way? And listen . . . no more meeting like this. Starting tomorrow night we've got the Reeves' apartment. (*Holds up two keys*) Matching keys, his and hers. (*Hands her one*) You may not like the paintings—lots of little orphans with big eyes. But we won't be looking at them much. (*Gives her a long hug and kiss*) I can't figure out what the hell you see in me.

> (*He exits through the stage door, and she lifts her hand to wave good-bye*)

EVE   (*Sighing happily, she looks around at the theater and then begins to sing "One Hallowe'en"*)
Remember that Hallowe'en
When you were nine?
You wore a fairy-queen costume of your own design . . .

Well, look at you now . . .

And you put on rouge and lipstick
Though it wasn't allowed,
You were so proud!
And Daddy said, "Wash your face,
You look like a whore,"
That's what he said,
No more.

And so you went upstairs,
Washed your face,
Took off the dress,
Threw it away,
Got into bed,
As though it were the end
Of an ordinary day . . .
And outside,
The moon continued to shine.

Remember that Hallowe'en
When you were nine?

Well, screw you, Daddy. Look at your little girl now!

*(Turns, puts the key on the chaise, then runs up the
spiral steps and stops to look down on the stage—
the world she is about to conquer)*

She feels twitchy and bitchy
And manic,
Calm and collected
And no sign of panic,
She's alive,
She's alive,
So alive!

(Starts moving down the steps)

I'm wound up like a spring
That's been tightened,
Dreamy and dizzy
But not a bit frightened,
I'm alive,
I'm alive,
So alive!

(Leaves the steps and walks toward the wings)

Ev'rybody loves a winner,
But nobody loves a flop!
No one worries how you got there
Once you're standing on the top!

(*Now faces forward*)

So I feel up and together
And steady,
Eager, excited,
So come on, I'm ready!
Ready for the climb,
Baby, it's my time!
You believe it, I'm
Alive! Alive!

(*She turns and picks up her bag, coat, and key.*
HOWARD *enters from the right*)

Howard!

HOWARD (*Casually*) Hello!

EVE (*Taken aback*) How long have you . . . ?

HOWARD (*Moving slowly toward her*) Long enough. I
came in through the front. Bert told me I might find you
here. I've never seen you caught off guard before.

EVE (*Standing at the end of the chaise, composed*) Howard,
there's nothing to hide. Something wonderful has happened to me. We've fallen in love! He's rewriting Leslie
for me . . . and, well . . . it's getting pretty serious. Of
course I feel awful about Karen . . .

HOWARD Yes, yes, of course—that makes it tough.

EVE *(Goes toward the stage door)* Well, I've got to go . . .

HOWARD If there's a wedding license, don't forget to write Evelyn Hinkle. That's your name, isn't it?

EVE *(Stopping)* Yes, what about it?

HOWARD I've done a bit of research on you. That whole pathetic-lost-soul autobiography. Very touching, but a complete lie, from beginning to end.

> (EVE *puts down her case and coat, and walks quickly back toward* HOWARD)

EVE I just *had* to get in to see Margo. I had to make them like me.

HOWARD They liked you all right. And what have you done for them in return? The bodies are piling up. I don't want mine among them.

EVE *(Defiantly)* Howard, Buzz and I—

HOWARD *(Taking her key)* Forget about "Buzz and I." It's "you and I."

EVE It *was* you and I, Howard . . . for one night. But with Buzz . . . I really love him.

HOWARD Don't you think your future with Buzz could be complicated by his hearing about your current activities? Hopscotch to the top, from bed to bed—Bert, Stan Harding, me.

EVE Buzz loves me. I can explain all that.

HOWARD   Really. Can you explain this simple fact: your husband wasn't killed in Vietnam. He's still there—alive!

(She looks at him coldly)

EVE   What do you want?

HOWARD *(Circling behind her, then moving back)* You, until I start yawning. I want you to let Buzz down gently. Take a week or so—I want a playwright, not a blubbering wreck. And then, if you're a very good girl, we'll see about the part in the play. Come here. *(She doesn't budge)* Come here. *(She walks over to him slowly. He takes her chin in his hand and kisses her)* Don't clench your teeth when I kiss you.

(He kisses her again, this time pulling back quickly and touching his lip. There is blood. He slaps her)

EVE *(Under her breath)*   Goddamn you. Goddamn you.

HOWARD   Eve, we both know what you want. And you know I can get it for you, don't you? . . . Don't you? *(Defeated, she nods)* Well, then. Here . . . *(He puts some money in her hand)* Take a taxi, get your things, and be at my place in an hour. And if I'm not there— wait.

(He exits. EVE stands there, stunned, unable to move)

SCENE SIX

It is a week later. The dressing-room set comes on, and MARGO, *in her dressing gown, is seen pacing.* PETER *is seated next to the dressing table, and* DUANE *is sitting on the sofa.*

PETER *(Soothingly)*   C'mon, sweetie, it's not the only part ever written . . . or the greatest. Now you just play out this run, take it on the road . . .

MARGO *(Still pacing, helplessly)*   Where *is* everybody? I asked for a meeting here after the matinee, not just you, but the whole office.

(*She goes to the bar*)

PETER   Well, the boss is in L.A., Bob's in London, and . . .

MARGO   And what's the point of it without Howard here?

PETER   He wouldn't return my call.

MARGO *(Moving to her chair, then pacing again, urgently)* You're not going to let Howard get away with this! It all comes from him. This is *my* part. It was written for me. It's always been understood.

PETER *(Following* MARGO *unhappily)*   The play's ready.

They're anxious to get it on, and we have no written contract . . .

MARGO   Buzz certainly couldn't have agreed to this (PETER *shrugs*) And Bill? Is he directing it? . . . With her?

PETER   You'd know better than anyone.

MARGO   Would I? Haven't seen him in weeks. That part was the only thing in my future. (*Looking lost*) Now where am I?

PETER   But, sweetie, it's not the end of the world.

MARGO   Maybe not for you. (*Looking around the dressing room, encompassing it with a gesture*) Get it straight, Peter. This is it. This is my whole life. (*Imploring*) Do something about it! (*He shrugs helplessly. She is resigned*) Go home and have a good dinner. You look awful.

PETER (*Touched*)   Thanks, Margo. G'night.

> (*He leaves.* DUANE *walks over to her, gives her a light kiss, and puts his arm around her shoulder*)

MARGO (*To* DUANE, *trying to smile*)   Hey, you're not going to be her hairdresser, are you?

DUANE   Only when she's laid out.

MARGO (*Overwhelmed again*)   How am I going to stop her?

DUANE   How can you when she's got the author in her pocket?

MARGO Hm?

DUANE Well . . . in her bed.

MARGO (*Stunned*) Buzz . . . and Eve?

DUANE It's practically been a headline in *Variety*.

(*The door opens.* KAREN *looks in*)

KAREN Margo?

MARGO Karen!

KAREN I'm glad you're still here. I'll tell the doorman to let the cab go.

(*She ducks out*)

DUANE Hey, look. I better cut out. See you at half-hour. And make sure you eat something. (*To* KAREN, *as she comes in and he is leaving*) Oh, hi, Mrs. Richards.

KAREN Hi, Duane.

MARGO (*Nervously trying to be offhand*) Hello . . . what's the good word? Uh . . . who said that? I never say things like that. Uh . . . you want a shrimp? Some steak? Can I get you a drink?

(KAREN *has the intense look of someone who has been drinking. She takes off her coat and puts the coat and her pocketbook on the sofa*)

KAREN   Yeah! Jack Daniels . . . cooking sherry . . . anything. Margo, justice is not dead!

MARGO (*Pouring a drink and taking it to* KAREN)   Oh, good.

KAREN   Retribution. Punishment for sins. I've been doing a lot of thinking.

MARGO   You mean *drink*ing.

KAREN   I wish I could get plotzed. All the time. Can't live with myself. Your little Radcliffee girl emptied that gas tank, loused up her friend, and now she's getting what she deserves . . . Didn't you hear me?

MARGO   I heard. You and the gas tank. It took me a whole day to figure that out. (*Puts her hands on* KAREN'*s shoulders*) I knew it was Eve pulling the strings.

KAREN   Margo, you were so right about—

MARGO   Yes, I win a lot of medals for being on to that girl. They're pinned right to my skin. I . . . just heard about Buzz.

KAREN (*Moving away*)   You marry a funny-looking, lovable little playwright, put him through college, sharpen his pencils, pretend to like his early plays, and then . . . suddenly . . . (*Stamping her foot, then breaking down*) I'll kill him! I'll kill them both! (*Weeping, she slumps into the chair near the dressing table*) Margo, help me!

(MARGO *goes over to* KAREN *and holds her*)

MARGO You've certainly come to an expert. I've lost every man who ever came into my life, including the only one I really loved.

KAREN What do we do?

MARGO I know exactly what *you* have to do. Nothing.

KAREN Huh?

MARGO Eve doesn't want your playwright husband. She wants his play.

KAREN She'd do all this for a part in a play?

MARGO Right. Sit still and wait.

KAREN Wait!

(*Gets up*)

That's no way to fight a woman like that!

MARGO (*Sitting* KAREN *back down*) Listen to me! On *this* subject, I really *am* an expert. Buzz is just one step up for her. Those dainty claws are already dug in for the next jump, and jump she will, no matter whose body is in the way. If she's talented, she'll get there. But *staying* up there—that's the backbreaker, the full time job. I almost feel sorry for Eve, because in the end she'll wind up empty and alone, married to herself, fighting for parts she's no longer right for . . . and . . . and no *won*der I'm such an expert on this subject. It's *me*!

KAREN *(Getting up and running to* MARGO*)*   No!

MARGO   You must admit there's a faint resemblance. And I don't like it. Karen, I've got to do something about it.

> *(They kiss.* KAREN *picks up her coat and pocketbook from the sofa)*

KAREN *(Excitedly)*   And I've got to go right home and . . . and . . . do nothing!

> *(They are at the door.* KAREN *goes, and* MARGO *follows her into the area outside the door)*

MARGO *(Stopping* KAREN*)*   Karen, got a good recipe for lasagna?

KAREN   What?

MARGO   I'll call you. (KAREN *exits.* MARGO *steps forward and with a growing sense of realization and urgency sings "Something Greater")*

> A scrapbook full of clippings
> Of things long forgotten,
> There's something greater!
>
> A picture in the paper
> That makes you look rotten,
> There's something greater!
>
> The meaningless attention,
> The bowing and the smirking
> Of some headwaiter . . .
>
> That lost and empty feeling

The nights that you're not working,
I know there's something better,
I know there's something greater!

A theater full of strangers
Adoring you blindly,
There's something greater,
There's something greater!

The friends who know you're lonely
And treat you too kindly,
There's something greater,
There's something greater!

There's needing to be where he is,
Waking up and there he is,
Being to your man what a woman should be!
That's something greater,
Something greater!
And, finally, that's for me!

(*The music continues to play as* MARGO *paces up
and down excitedly. The dressing-room set goes off,
revealing the backstage set*)

SCENE SEVEN

Backstage. As MARGO *paces, the lights dim. At the opposite side of the stage, a spotlight picks up* BILL. MARGO *turns and sees him.*

BILL *(Moving toward* MARGO, *singing)*
There's needing to be where she is,
Waking up and there she is . . .

MARGO *(Moving toward him, singing)*
Being to your man what a woman should be!

(The music continues in the background)

Bill, I'm sorry.

BILL *I'm* sorry. I should have protected you from that girl. She's a—

MARGO *(Putting her hand over his mouth)* Don't say a word against her. And let the kid have the part. If it weren't for her, I would have lost you. *(Looking out to the front with a happy grin, and calling)* Eve! You four-star bitch! Thank you!

BILL and MARGO *(Singing)*
That's something greater!
Something greater!
And, finally, that's for me!
(They turn, walk upstage, and embrace)

Curtain

About the Authors

BETTY COMDEN and ADOLPH GREEN are triply talented as authors, lyricists and performers. As a team, they occupy a unique place in stage and screen history. In *Applause,* for the first time they have focused on the writing of only the book, which received extraordinary critical acclaim. Their additional satisfaction in *Applause* was writing for their close friend Lauren Bacall and seeing her emerge, after all her years of fame, as the most exciting discovery on Broadway. They have a formidable record of achievement in both theater and motion pictures: Tony Awards for *Wonderful Town, Hallelujah, Baby!* and *Applause;* Screen Writers' Guild Awards for *The Bandwagon, On the Town, Singin' in the Rain* and *It's Always Fair Weather,* as well as three Oscar nominations. Their theater contributions include *On the Town, Bells Are Ringing, Billion Dollar Baby, Subways Are for Sleeping,* Mary Martin's *Peter Pan* and *Do Re Mi.*

Both native New Yorkers, Miss Comden and Mr. Green began their careers as performers in a pioneering satirical act with Judy Holliday called *The Revuers.* They performed again in the first Broadway show they wrote, *On the Town,* and later in *A Party,* a one-man, one-woman show composed of material from their Broadway musicals and movies, which won an Obie Award for the best off-Broadway musical of the season.

Miss Comden and her husband, Steven Kyle, have two children, Susanna and Alan. Mr. Green and his wife, Phyllis Newman, have two children, Adam and Amanda. Both families live in New York.

CHARLES STROUSE and LEE ADAMS burst upon Broadway in 1960 with their music and lyrics for the smash hit *Bye, Bye, Birdie,* which won the Tony Award for Best Musical. Since then, the team has been busy with Broadway musicals *(All American, Golden Boy, Superman, Applause)* and motion pictures. Charles Strouse composed the score for the prize-winning *Bonnie and Clyde,* and Mr. Strouse and Mr. Adams received acclaim for their songs in the movie *The Night They Raided Minsky's.* Their most recent film is *There Was a Crooked Man.* Among the over four hundred Strouse-Adams songs are: "A Lot of Livin' to Do," "Put on a Happy Face," "You've Got Possibilities," "Kids," "Once Upon a Time," "Night Song," "I Want to Be with You," "This Is the Life," and, now, "Applause." They are currently working on the score for the film *The Borrowers.*

Mr. Strouse is married to the former Barbara Siman. They live in his native New York with their sons Benjamin and Nicholas. Mr. Adams makes his home in Connecticut with his wife, Rita, and daughter, Diane.